Scroll Saw Segmentation

Patterns, Projects & Techniques

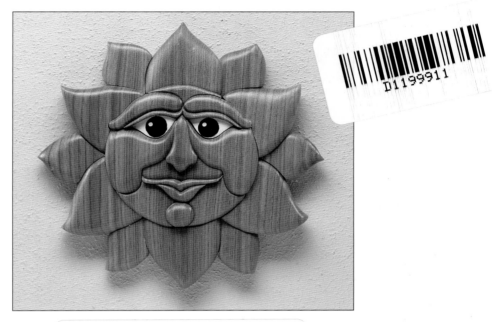

Scroll Saw Segmentation

Patterns, Projects & Techniques

Patrick Spielman

Sterling Publishing Co., Inc. New York
A Sterling/Chapelle Book

Chapelle Ltd.
Owner: Jo Packham

Editor: Leslie Ridenour

Staff: Marie Barber, Ann Bear, Kass Burchett, Rebecca Christensen, Marilyn Goff, Holly Hollingsworth, Susan Jorgensen, Barbara Milburn, Linda Orton, Karmen Quinney, Cindy Stoeckl, Gina Swapp

Photographer: Kevin Dilley for Hazen Photography

Acknowledgments From the Author

First, a special thanks to my talented wife, Patricia, for creating and painting most of the projects, and helping me with a variety of chores related to preparing this book. A hearty thanks to Albert F. Winberg, who graciously permitted me to include his wonderful intarsia pieces and original patterns. Designs and patterns provided by Bev Carmody, Frank Droege, Aaron Moriarity, R. Stephan Toman, Joan West, and Terry Wolf add "spice" and variety to the reader's choices of projects. Thanks also to graphic artist, Roxanne LeMoine, and typists, Jenny Blahnik and Chris Milton, for their efforts and expedient assistance.

Library of Congress Cataloging-in-Publication Data

Spielman, Patrick E.
    Scroll saw segmentation : patterns, projects & techniques / Patrick Spielman.
      p. cm.
    "A Sterling/Chapelle book."
    ISBN 0-8069-1907-8
    1. Jig saws. 2. Woodwork--Patterns. I. Title.

TT186 .S67417 2000
745. 51'3--dc21

99-059785

10 9 8 7 6 5 4 3 2 1

A Sterling/Chapelle Book

Published by Sterling Publishing Company, Inc.
387 Park Avenue South, New York, NY 10016
© 2000 by Chapelle Ltd.
Distributed in Canada by Sterling Publishing
% Canadian Manda Group, One Atlantic Avenue, Suite 105
Toronto, Ontario, Canada M6K 3E7
Distributed in Great Britain and Europe by Cassell PLC
Wellington House, 125 Strand, London WC2R 0BB, England
Distributed in Australia by Capricorn Link (Australia) Pty Ltd.
P.O. Box 6651, Baulkham Hills, Business Centre, NSW 2153, Australia
Printed in China
All Rights Reserved

Sterling ISBN 0-8069-1907-8

If you have any questions or comments, please contact:

Chapelle Ltd., Inc.
P.O. Box 9252
Ogden, UT 84409
Phone: (801) 621-2777
FAX: (801) 621-2788
e-mail: Chapelle1@ChapelleLtd.com

Pat Spielman can be reached via his website or e-mail:

http: www.spielmanpatrick.com
e-mail: spielman@mail.wiscnet.net

Contents

Introduction 6
Segmentation versus Intarsia 6
Advantages of Segmentation....................7

Chapter 1 8
Scroll Saws 8
Blades..10

Chapter 2 12
Wood Materials..12
Plywood & Sheet Materials 13

Chapter 3 14
Basic Techniques & Tools..........................14
Proceed with Safety 14
Prepare the Saw 15
Basic Tools & Supplies 15
Segmentation Technique Instructions....16

Chapter 4: Segmented Fish 29
Striped Fish 29
Pink & Blue Fish 31
Speckled Fish 33

Chapter 5: Segmented Birds 35
Two-piece Shore Bird 35
Four-piece Sea Gull 37
Carved Duck..39
Duck Decoy 41
Swan 43
Road Runner..45

Chapter 6: Halloween & Thanksgiving....49
Pumpkin & Ghost 49
Holiday Turkey 51

Chapter 7: Christmas 53
Santa Face 53
Angel..55
Nativity 57
Madonna & Child 59

Chapter 8: Fantasy 61
Sun Face..61
Moon Face 64
Unicorn..67

Chapter 9: Nautical Projects................70
Mermaid 70
Lighthouse 72
Antique Anchor 75
Sculpted Sailboat 78
Making Rope-edged Plaques 80

Chapter 10: Nostalgic Projects............84
First Kiss 84
Big Catch 86
Woman with Basket 89

Chapter 11: Country Projects 91
Small Rooster..91
Rooster Plaques 93
Segmented Sunflower................................96
Segmented Pony..99

Chapter 12: Home Decor......................101
Heart in Home 102
Segmented Mirror 104

Chapter 13: Separated Segmentation 106
Luv Bugs 106
Segmented Butterfly 109
Viking 113

Chapter 14: Intarsia Segmentation....115
Intarsia Rosebud 115
Intarsia Santa 117
Umbrella Man & Woman 120
Shell Box 123

Metric Equivalency Chart....................127
Index 128

Introduction

This book is about employing the fine-line cutting capability of the scroll saw in combination with some elementary wood-shaping techniques to make decorative woodworking pieces that appear to be artfully carved. The resulting sculptural-looking pieces appear to require much more advanced and masterful skills than they actually do. See Photos No. i-1 and No. i-2. This art or craft, which I call "segmentation," can be learned in a reasonably short time by anyone of any age and ability level.

Photo No. i-1   Segmentation projects are shown with an all-natural finish (left) and some segments stained (right).

Photo No. i-2   Here, segmentation finishing incorporates a variety of options: natural, stained, and colored with acrylic paints. See pages 93–95 for Rooster Plaques patterns.

I introduced the essential techniques of scroll saw segmentation more than 12 years ago. Since that time, I have included many segmentation projects in my various scroll saw pattern/project books and in my bimonthly magazine, *Home Workshop News*. This book is basically a compilation of those projects.

Segmentation versus Intarsia

During the last decade, "segmentation" and a more advanced level of essentially the same process, called "intarsia," have steadily grown. See Photo No. i-3 on opposite page. Segmentation is sometimes referred to as "painted intarsia." Intarsia is also called "3-D marquetry," or "3-D inlay." The techniques involved in these two processes are very similar. Both art forms can be carried to various levels of sophistication (or difficulty) to create beautifully dimensioned flat-backed sculptures. Both segmentation and intarsia impart a visual quality of low-relief carving but with the addition of various painted colors or a range of natural wood tones. This is what makes this work so desirable and intriguing. The results emulate fine carving, but the work is much easier to accomplish and therein lies the fun and enjoyment of this exciting woodworking activity.

However, there are also some distinct differences between the two. Segmentation projects are, as a rule, made from just one board or a single piece of inexpensive material. The process simply involves cutting out patterns of objects, such as fish, animals, scenery, and the like, into primary elements, or segments (tails, wings, legs, etc.), separating them from the whole. The edges or surfaces of each part are rounded over or otherwise contoured and shaped with hand or power tools. A pigmented color, stain, or natural finish is applied to the individual segments. Lastly, the segments are reassembled with wood glue to re-create the whole. There are many finishing and painting options available for segmentation projects. See Photos No. i-1 and No. i-2 on opposite page.

Intarsia, on the other hand, requires selecting stock from many different boards or pieces of wood in different natural colors—usually in dark-, medium-, and light-toned combinations. See Photo No. i-3.

Photo No. i-3   Examples of intarsia work show the use of all-natural wood colors provided by selecting appropriate varieties of different wood species. Shown is the design and work of noted intarsia author and artist Lucille Crabtree.

Sometimes one to a dozen or more different species of wood are used to make up the colors for the individual segments. Walnut and maple, for example, provide a dark brown and white that may be combined with various pink shades of Western cedar to create a colorful palette. Usually clear, natural finishes are used.

Each piece of wood selected for an intarsia project is chosen specifically for its natural color as well as its figure, or grain, direction, which complements the general design effect. Each segment of intarsia, however, is cut individually and must be made to fit precisely against the adjoining segments. Thus, in addition to using more expensive materials, intarsia is more labor-intensive and somewhat more difficult to accomplish overall.

Advantages of Segmentation

- Segmentation is an easier and faster process, usually requiring just a single piece of material.
- The process uses readily available and less expensive materials.
- Projects can be finished in a variety of ways: painting; staining; leaving natural; or any combination thereof.
- The ability to paint segments individually when separated eliminates cutting in blending and shading of colors.
- Individual patterns can be worked to various levels of difficulty. All scroll-sawn edges, for example, can be chamfered, rounded over slightly with sandpaper, or rounded over to a full radius equal to the material's thickness.
- Sanding requirements to smooth wood are not as critical when preparing for pigmented finishes as they are for clear, natural wood finishes.
- Segmentation provides good background and skill development experience necessary before undertaking intarsia projects.
- Beyond the use of a scroll saw, few tools are needed to get started.

For those new to this work, I have included basic information about scroll saws and various wood-shaping and smoothing tools that may be used. Also included are some recommendations concerning the selection of materials and an overview of the essential techniques involved to make the scroll saw segmentation projects presented in this book.

– Patrick Spielman

7

Chapter 1

Scroll Saws

The scroll saw is used to cut flat wood into distinct parts or segments. See Photo No. 1-1. Almost any scroll saw that carries fine blades (and that includes most scroll saws available today) can be used for segmentation work. This chapter provides essential information about scroll saws for the beginner and illustrates just a few of the more than 50 different machines on the market today.

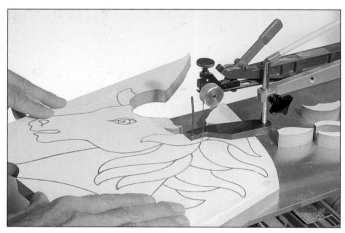

Photo No. 1-1   The scroll saw can cut a single ¾"-thick board into specific segments, using a No. 5 ground blade.

When compared to all other power-driven devices that cut wood, the scroll saw is unquestionably the safest, most user-friendly, and easiest to master. Scroll sawing is enjoyed by crafters and artists of all ages. It requires no mechanical skills and it allows for safely cutting small pieces of wood to quickly make a variety of projects. The major function of the scroll saw is to cut irregular curves and openings in flat wood. A very small, thin blade is held taut between the ends of two horizontal arms that move in unison up and down to create a reciprocating cutting motion. See Photos No. 1-2 and No. 1-3. The blade moves vertically through an opening in the saw table. The operator supports the work piece on the table and advances it into the blade in a manner that is similar to feeding fabric under the needle of a sewing machine.

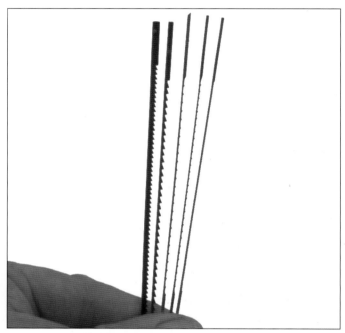

Photo No. 1-2   Scroll saws carry narrow blades. Although narrower blades than these are available, you will not need any finer than these for general work. Use wider blades with fewer teeth for cutting larger curves and cutting thicker woods; use narrower blades with more teeth for intricate details in thin woods.

Photo No. 1-3   Blades are clamped at each end to the upper arm, and to the lower arm under the table. A very important feature of scroll saw usage is its capability for installing and changing blades quickly and easily.

Because of the very narrow blades, extremely sharp arcs and turns can be cut to make highly detailed and intricate objects. To the uneducated and untrained eye, many people think that scrollwork is created with a laser.

Scroll saws are available in a wide variety of prices, ranging from less than $100.00 to well over $2,000.00, with a growing list of features and options that improve the overall performance of the machine. Many projects in this book can be made using any scroll saw, including the least expensive.

There are many saw brands to choose from and some manufacturers offer several models. Before purchasing any scroll saw, seriously consider the full range of work that might be done in the future. Scroll saws can cut a wide variety of materials, including various metals and plastics. Some scroll saws have more capability and capacity to cut thicker and larger sizes of wood than do others. Thus, it is necessary to investigate and try various saws, to see which saw best matches long-term cutting needs. For a more in-depth description of scroll saw usage and features, the previously published Sterling books, *Scroll Saw Basics* and *Scroll Saw Handbook* are recommended.

The size of the scroll saw is designated by its "throat capacity." This is the distance from the blade to the rear of the machine. A 15" saw, for example, can cut to the center of a 30"-diameter circle. Saw sizes range from 13" to 30" and are available in bench and floor model versions.

The rate at which the blade moves up and down in strokes per minute is called the "blade speed." The least expensive saws have just one constant speed. Two-speed and variable-speed saws allow for better control when cutting thin or soft materials, as well as the ability to efficiently cut metal and plastic.

The photos included here provide a good overview of some popular brands of saws that are now available. See Photos No. 1-4 through No. 1-9 below and on page 10.

Photo No. 1-4   Delta's two-speed 16" scroll saw is one of several models available from the manufacturer and costs about $175.

Photo No. 1-5   Ryobi's 16" variable-speed scroll saw costs about $170 without the magnifier light.

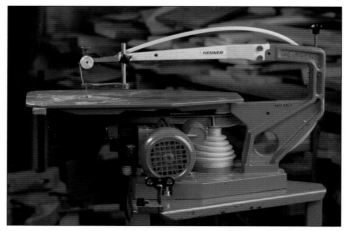

Photo No. 1-6   This Hegner, a German-made 18" variable-speed machine, features up-front tensioning and costs about $1,000.

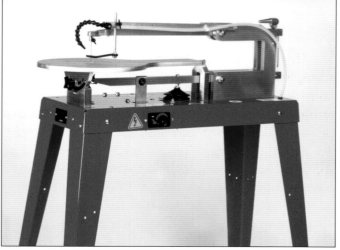

Photo No. 1-9   The RBI Hawk is a 26" variable-speed saw with up-front tensioning. It is made in America and costs about $1,200.

In addition to considering variable-speed saws, some saw features worth considering are up-front controls, i.e.: an on-off switch, blade tensioning, and blade speed adjustment. Look into adaptability, i.e.: possibility of adding a light, a magnifier, a dust collector, and/or a blower. A foot switch is another good optional accessory. Remember, the most important feature to look for is the saw's capacity for changing blades quickly and/or threading the blade through the work piece easily for making inside cuts. See Photo No. 1-3 on page 8.

Photo No. 1-7   DeWalt is made in Canada. It is a 20" variable-speed saw and one of the newest brands available. It has many innovative features and costs about $475.

Blades

Blades are fairly inexpensive, costing between 20 to 75 cents each, depending upon size, style, quantity, and quality. The most popular blade is the 5" plain-end type. Sizes are designated by numbers and range from No. 2/0 and No. 0 in very fine, to No. 1, No. 2, and No. 4 in fine, to No. 5 to No. 7 in medium, and No. 8 to No. 12 in large sizes. Photo No. 1-2 on page 8 illustrates some medium- and fine-sized blades.

Photo No. 1-8   Excalibur, also made in Canada, is a 30" variable-speed saw. It has the largest throat capacity available and costs about $1,400.

The slight forward and back movement of the blade during the cutting stroke of the scroll saw produces a cut surface that is smooth and seldom needs sanding.

There are various blade tooth design configurations available, with skip-tooth being one of the most popular. See Drawing No. 1-1. This blade tooth design provides for fast sawdust removal and provides cool and smooth cuts. Look for blades with reversed lower teeth. These minimize tear-out or splintering as the teeth exit the bottom of the work piece.

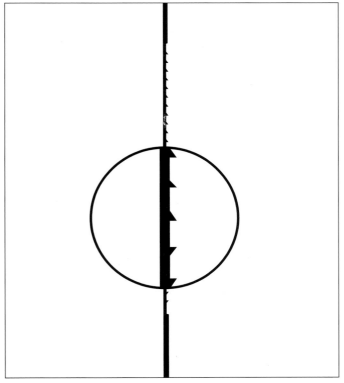

Drawing No. 1-1   Skip-tooth design with reversed lower teeth minimizes bottom splintering or feathering along the cut edges of the piece.

Less expensive blades have burr edges along one side. See Drawing No. 1-2. The burr edge is the result of material flow from stamping or milling during manufacturing. The burr-edged side of the blade is sharper and provides less cutting resistance than the burrless side of the blade. This causes the blade to track slightly to one side while cutting—a condition for which one can quickly learn to compensate. The side-tracking tendency of these blades is especially noticeable when making straight line cuts.

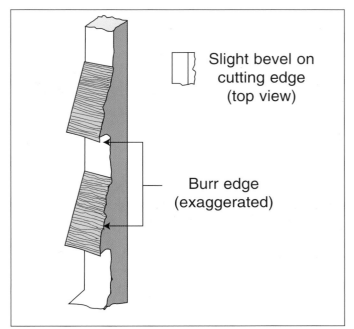

Slight bevel on cutting edge (top view)

Burr edge (exaggerated)

Drawing No. 1-2   This enlarged sketch shows the sharp, microscopic metal burr along one edge of the blade. This condition is typical of less expensive scroll saw blades. It is caused by the way the blades are manufactured. For this reason, scroll saw blades actually track unevenly, because there is more cutting resistance on one edge of the blade than the other.

The best, newest, and most expensive blades are ground from tempered steel with abrasive wheels. These are known as "ground blades." They last longer and cut straighter when compared to other blades.

Use ground blades for the smoothest-cut surfaces. They stay sharp longer when cutting plywoods and also make smooth cuts in pine. Avoid spiral blades. Although designed to cut in all directions, they are not a good choice for beginners. They cut slowly, take a wide kerf, and leave a very rough-cut surface.

For general softwood cutting, use larger blades: No. 7 to No. 12 for ¾" and thicker stock. Use No. 5 to No. 7 for ½" to ¾" stock, and No. 1 to No. 5 for ⅛" to ½" stock. Just three blades—No. 2, No. 4, and No. 5—are recommended to handle most of the cutting projects in this book.

Chapter 2

Wood Materials

A broad range of wood materials with different characteristics may be used for segmentation projects. Choices include soft to hard, light to dark, inexpensive to expensive, thin to thick, common to exotic, natural to painted, and so on. When making wood choices, it is important to keep in mind a few considerations.

Solid wood is categorized as hardwood or softwood. The best choice of any wood is, by and large, dictated by the specific end use. Sometimes physical hardness is important; however, it is not a major consideration for segmented projects.

Common hardwoods include ash, beech, birch, cherry, maple, oak, and pecan. Mahogany, poplar, and walnut might be considered medium-hard.

Typical softwoods include basswood, butternut, cedars, cypress, firs, pines, redwood, and spruce. See Photos No. 2-1 and No. 2-2.

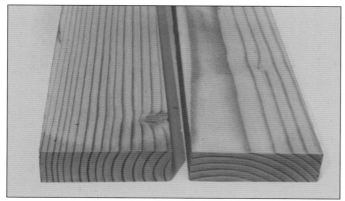

Photo No. 2-1   A general rule for all wood: Quarter-sawn boards, like the one on the left, will stay flatter and distort less than the plain-sawn boards on the right. Note the different figure, or grain, patterns from the growth rings. These examples are of Douglas fir—not a recommended choice for segmentation projects as it tends to splinter and is also difficult to smooth.

Photo No. 2-2   Inexpensive No. 2 shop pine is often a good choice for small projects that can be cut out around defects. Boards may be found flat like the one on the left, but usually wide plain-sawn boards will have some distortion and cupping, like the boards at the lower right. Note the typical knot and pitch pockets, which are areas that should be avoided.

Then there are the exotic woods, such as padauk, purpleheart, zebrawood, and many others. Most exotic woods are considered to be hard rather than soft and are almost always quite expensive. Exotic woods are not recommended for any project in this book.

When a natural finish is desired, woods should be selected for their color and figure, or grain, patterns. It is important to understand that different grain patterns result from the way the board is cut from the log. See Photo No. 2-1. If the project will be stained or painted, almost any wood will serve. However, the prudent choice is an inexpensive softwood or a remanufactured sheet material, such as plywood or MDF.

The various materials used for the samples of the projects in this book are, in fact, only a small sampling of suitable materials available. Check with a local supplier for available species, pricing, and other options.

Tip

Purchasing less costly, lower grades of wood justifies cutting from clear areas between defects.

Consider the possibility of positioning patterns around problem areas, such as knots. Discolored boards (those with blue-stain, etc.) are fine to use when a project will be painted—as long as there is no decay—as their surfaces will be hidden anyway. If you own a table saw and a jointer, you can utilize clear, narrower, boards and glue them edge to edge to make wider pieces. See Photo No. 2-3.

Photo No. 2-3   Clear pieces, ripped to remove defects, are glued edge to edge to make a wide board.

Plywood & Sheet Materials

Some plywoods and certain sheet materials offer advantages over solid boards. They do not check or crack. They stay flat, are strong in all directions, do not swell or shrink, and are available in larger sizes. Generally, they also have uniform surface characteristics with minimal waste. However, as a rule, sheet materials manufactured for utility work and building construction should not be used for scroll saw segmentation projects.

Some sheet materials cost less than solid woods. But others, such as fine hardwood plywoods, can be extremely expensive. Highly ornate and delicate designs are less fragile when cut from plywood. Baltic birch plywood, for example, has sound inner plies and is a popular choice for general scroll saw segmentation cutting. The thinner pieces, ⅛"- to ¼"-thick, make excellent backers.

Medium density fiberboard (MDF) is an engineered wood sheet material, which is made from lumbering leftovers: chips, sawdust, plywood trimmings, etc. See Photo No. 2-4. MDF is free of knots, has no grain direction, is flat, and has a uniformly homogenous construction from surface to surface. MDF is a bit harder on saw blades and it also generates fine dust when cut, so always use a dust mask when cutting MDF.

Photo No. 2-4   Left: Poplar plywoods and Baltic birch plywoods, in thinner sheets, are good for scroll sawing because of their void-free interiors and smooth surfaces. Baltic birch plywoods thicker than ⅜" may cause blade dulling problems because of the abrasiveness of all the glue. Right: piece of MDF (medium density fiberboard).

Do not confuse MDF with particleboard. Particleboard has tough, hard, tool-dulling resins. It is also made from lumbering wastes that are only mechanically reduced to chips. MDF is wood reduced to individual fibers. The manufacturing of it involves a combination of steaming and chemical processes.

MDF is not commonly used, but is a good choice for painted work, if it can be found. MDF is not very pretty unless painted. A building project supplier in your area may be able to order a 4' x 8' sheet. MDF is fairly inexpensive, costing about half the price of No. 2 shop pine. Check it out at your local supplier. Maybe you will be fortunate enough to find a local cabinet maker who uses it.

13

Chapter 3

Basic Techniques & Tools

Nearly every woodworking task can be performed in more than one way—hand tool versus power tool techniques is one common comparison. This chapter will explain the basic technique for making the projects and illustrate a variety of hand and power tools, plus some different ways in which they may be used to achieve similar results.

Proceed with Safety

The process of using and understanding any power tool will contribute to the success and sense of accomplishment that come with a job well done.

However, one should proceed with caution as the materials used by a craftsperson can be dangerous and potentially lethal. The combination of potentially noxious dust, harmful chemicals and paints, high noise levels, sharp tools, and high quantities of electricity, make it imperative that the craftsperson operates a safe, clean, and well thought-out environment. See Photos No. 3-1 and No. 3-2. The risk of injury should never be underestimated.

Photo No. 3-1   This scroll saw set-up vacuums away dust from above the work piece and also below the table. The vacuum and saw operate simultaneously with the single foot switch.

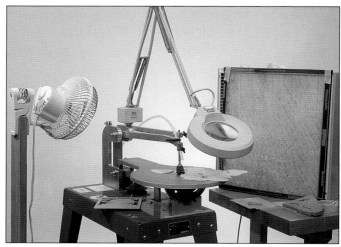

Photo No. 3-2   An alternative to vacuum removal of dust is the use of a square household fan with a furnace filter taped to it to collect fine air-born dust. A second small fan, positioned opposite the saw and filter, contributes to the air flow. Use this same set-up with routers, power sanders, and rotary tools.

Remember the following safety guidelines:

- Understand and strictly observe rules with regard to the manufacturer's instructions in the safe operation of all tools.
- Always wear a respirator or dust mask while working.
- Wear eye and ear protection when working with power tools.
- Never allow fingers to come near any moving blades or cutters.
- Wear appropriate attire, such as a shop apron—no jewelry and no loose sleeves or ties.
- Feel comfortable when using power tools. Think out your project in its entirety and understand all aspects of it before beginning.
- Always keep your mind on your work. Do not allow your mind to wander or be distracted when using power tools or sharp objects.
- Above all, never work when tired, in a hurry, or not in the mood. Put the project down for today and come back to it later, in a better

frame of mind and with time to spare. Use common sense at all times and each and every new challenging project or idea will be equally satisfying.

Prepare the Saw

Make certain to first read and review the owner's manual and observe all of the safety precautions relative to the use of the scroll saw. For most of the projects, it is necessary to make cuts with the saw table set square to the blade. Use a small square or protractor to make and check this adjustment. The factory calibrations on the blade-tilt scales of most scroll saws are difficult to read (especially with bifocals) and most are not accurate. See Photo No. 3-3. Make certain that the blade is installed with the teeth pointing downward. Tension it correctly, according to the manufacturer's instructions.

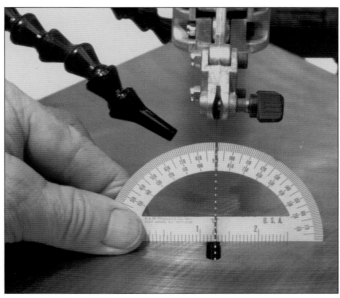

Photo No. 3-3   Using a simple protractor is the easiest way to check the squareness of the table to the blade and to adjust table tilt to the desired angle for bevel cutting.

Basic Tools & Supplies

Acrylic paints
Adhesive spray: temporary bonding aerosol
Blades
Brads: small
Carving knives
Chisels
Colored dyes: transparent
Colored paints: opaque
Copy paper
Cotton cloth
Craft knife
Craft scissors
Dowels
Drill and drill bits
Emery boards
Files
Flutter wheel: 150 or 180 grit
Finish: natural
Paintbrushes
Paper towels
Pencil
Picture frame hangers: sawtooth
Pliers
Plywood: ⅛"- to ¼"-thick for waste backers
Proportion scale
Rasps
Rotary tool: high-speed with various accessories
Sanders: belt or disk with coarse abrasives, 36 to 50
     or 60 grit; drum; orbital
Sandpaper
Scroll sanders
Scroll saw
Sponge brushes
Square or protractor: small
Stains: colored; oil
Tack cloth
Tape: double-sided
Trim router and bits
Waxed paper, freezer paper, or plastic wrap
Wood-burning tool
Wood glue (yellow carpenter's glue) or instant/super
     glues

Segmentation Technique Instructions

Unless otherwise specified in individual project instructions, construct segmentation and intarsia projects using the following technique instructions:

I. Prepare the Patterns.

1. Select the wood. Sand and smooth the surface and remove excess dust with a tack cloth.

2. Determine if the pattern will be used as presented in the book or if size adjustments need to be made. Consider also the sizes of selected wood to be used for the project(s) selected. (A slight size reduction of the pattern may allow for refitting it onto a piece of wood that would otherwise be cast aside.) Use a proportion scale to help determine the exact percentage of reduction or enlargement required before making a photocopy of the pattern. See Photo No. 3-4.

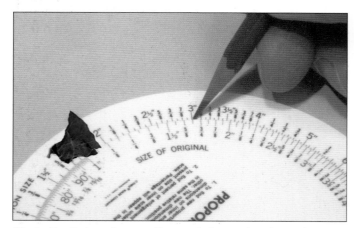

Photo No. 3-4   A proportion scale is used to determine optimum sizes when reducing or enlarging patterns on a photocopy machine. Simply align the mark indicating the existing size of the pattern in the book, then turn the scale to the desired finished size and take note of the percentage in the window. Set the copy machine to the percentage designated in the proportion scale's window.

3. Reduce or enlarge the pattern to any size desired at a copy shop or using an available copy machine.

4. Make two photocopies of the pattern—one for cutting and the other to use later to assemble the segments on.

5. Using scissors, cut the excess paper from around one copy of the pattern, leaving about ½" beyond the shape of the design. The wood should be slightly larger than the copy.

6. Spray the back of the copy with adhesive spray. Allow to dry about 30 seconds and hand-press the copy to the face surface of the wooden work piece. The work piece is now ready for cutting. See Photo No. 3-5.

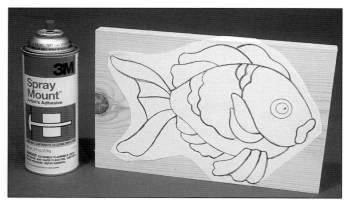

Photo No. 3-5   Adhere a photocopy of the pattern to the wood with temporary bond adhesive spray applied to the back of the pattern only.

II. Cut the Wood.

For beginners, making some preliminary cuts is recommended until confidence is gained and various lines can be followed consistently. See Photo No. 3-6 on the opposite page. The most difficult types of cuts to make accurately are perfectly straight lines, a true radius or full circle, and other geometric shapes, such as ovals, squares, and any parallel lines that run close together. See Photo No. 3-7 on the opposite page. Patience and practice are the keys to developing cutting skills.

Beginners should also use the hold-down and guard. Making quick, sharp, "on-the-spot" turns to cut inside corners and acute angles requires some practice and a fairly narrow blade.

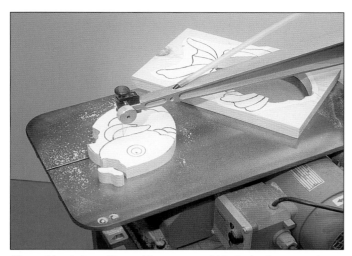

Photo No. 3-6   Use a No. 5 ground blade for best results when cutting the segments.

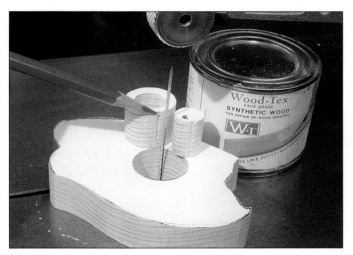

Photo No. 3-7   Small holes are drilled to cut out these concentric circular segments of a fish eye. The hole slots made by the drill can be hidden with wood filler and paint.

1. Cut out the segments. For most projects, the pattern provides thin cutting lines to follow. Cut either directly on the line or slightly to one side of it. However, take care not to cut too far outside the line as the integrity of the design may be spoiled.

2. For projects that have inside segments that must be cut out, simply drill a very small hole through the work piece in an inconspicuous place. Thread the blade through the hole in the work piece, reattach it to the saw and begin cutting.

3. Remove the paper pattern from the segments.

Tips

Cut plywood that is ¼"-thick and thinner on a slow-speed saw. If a slow-speed saw is not available, add extra stability to the project by using a waste-backer nailed, glued, or affixed with double-sided tape under the work piece. A waste-backer adds "blade resistance," resulting in better cutting control. The waste-backer also minimizes tear-out and splintering on the bottom of the work piece. Previously used plywood or paneling makes an effective and inexpensive waste-backer material.

When securing a waste-backer under the work piece with nails, drive small brads through the waste areas of both pieces while held over a flat piece of metal. See Photo No. 3-8. The metal will peen the nails on the bottom side. This technique works well with plywood as thin as ¹⁄₃₂"-thick.

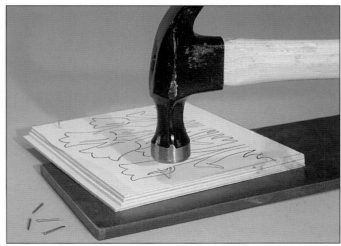

Photo No. 3-8   Stack-cutting is cutting two or more layers of materials at the same time. Here, the pieces are tacked together with brads driven through the waste areas while held over a flat piece of metal.

The same techniques can be employed when stack-cutting. Stack-cutting is a good production technique as it involves placing two or more layers, one on top of the other, securing them together so they do not slip or shift, and cutting all layers at once.

III. Shape & Smooth the Wood.

There are various fundamental shaping requirements for individual segments. Most projects involve chamfered or rounded-over edges. See Drawing No. 3-1 and Photo No. 3-9. Some projects, however, will look more interesting if formed to tapered, concave, or convex surfaces before working the edges. See Photo No. 3-10 and Drawing No. 3-2. Most woodworkers probably already have their own favorite devices or tools they like to use to shape wood.

Choose one or a combination of the following techniques:

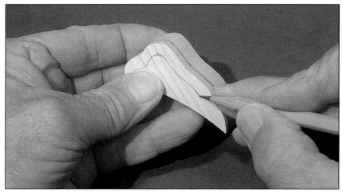

Photo No. 3-9   Finger-gauge a line to guide the round-over of an edge.

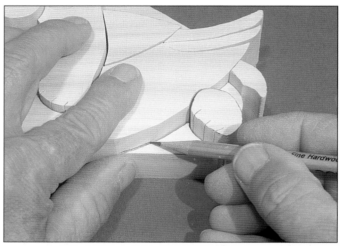

Photo No. 3-10   Where different levels or thicknesses exist, shape the lower segments first. Draw guide lines on adjoining segments to facilitate contouring so they appear to flow together as if carved from one piece.

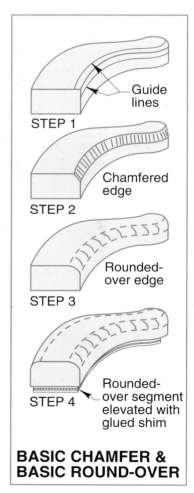

BASIC CHAMFER & BASIC ROUND-OVER

Drawing No. 3-1   These are the essential steps to shaping the edges of segments.

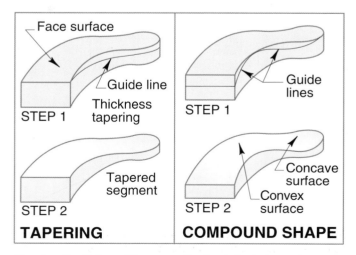

TAPERING   **COMPOUND SHAPE**

Drawing No. 3-2   These are the basic techniques for shaping the surfaces of segments.

1. Shape the segments using hand tools. Use sandpaper wrapped around a thin wooden tongue depressor, a dowel, or a pencil for minimal edge shaping and most smoothing jobs. See Photos No. 3-11 through No. 3-13. Use files, rasps, carving knives, and chisels to round-over cut edges or for giving other shapes to cut segments. See Photos No. 3-14 and No. 3-15.

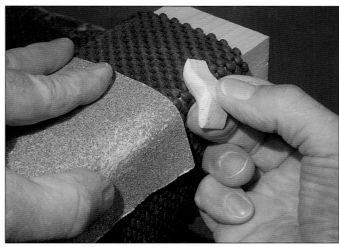

Photo No. 3-13   Rubbing an edge of a segment against a 60- or 80-grit abrasive held over a padded corner of the workbench will round-over and smooth small segments nicely.

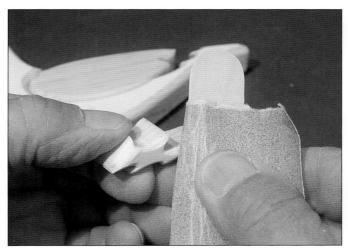

Photo No. 3-11   Sandpaper wrapped around a tongue depressor makes an effective file for rounding over edges of concave curves and in tight areas.

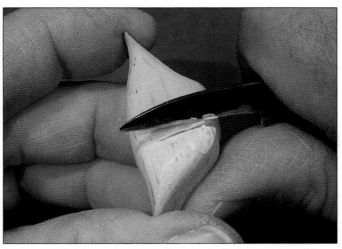

Photo No. 3-14   A rasp, a file, or a knife may be used to carve in detail, such as this fish's mouth.

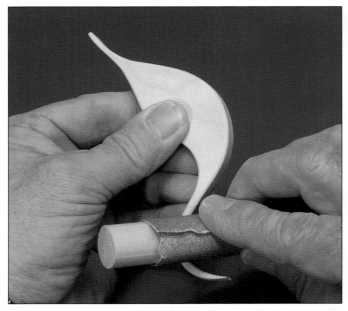

Photo No. 3-12   Sandpaper around a dowel or any round object, such as a pencil, is useful for rounding over edges of concave curves.

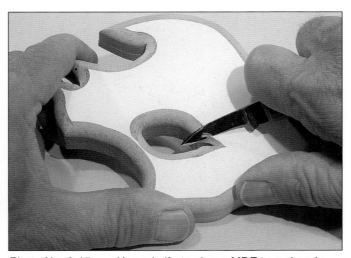

Photo No. 3-15   Use a knife to shape MDF to a sharply rounded inside corner of a unicorn's eye.

19

2. Shape the segments using rotary tools. Use high-speed rotary tools to tackle a variety of shaping and surface detailing jobs. Various accessories in different profiles and sizes are available for abrasive cutting and grinding of wood. See Photos No. 3-16 through No. 3-18.

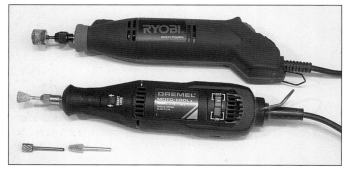

Photo No. 3-16   Small high-speed rotary tools can be fitted with a variety of cutting, shaping, and smoothing accessories.

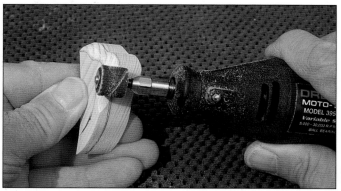

Photo No. 3-17   Round-over an edge with a small, coarse-grit sanding drum.

Photo No. 3-18   Carve a surface depression with a structured carbide burr.

You may need to use some innovative methods to safely hold very small segments for edge or surface shaping with hand and/or power tools. See Photos No. 3-19 through No. 3-22 below and on the opposite page. Use pliers or temporarily adhere the segment to a holding stick (dowel) with hot glue or double-sided tape. Obviously, you cannot safely hold small segments with your fingers. See Photos No. 3-23 and No. 3-24 on the opposite page.

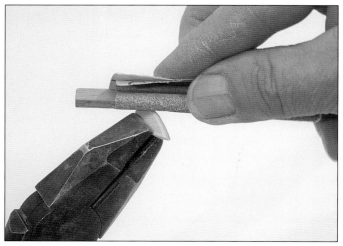

Photo No. 3-19   Hold a small thin segment with side-cutting pliers while rounding the edges by hand with an abrasive.

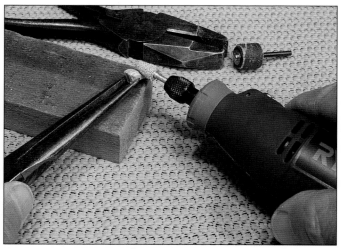

Photo No. 3-20   Needle-nose pliers grip a small segment while it is shaped on a supporting block with a rotary tool.

Photo No. 3-21   Temporarily bond the segment to a holding stick with double-sided tape or hot glue as the segment is worked against a drill press drum sander.

Photo No. 3-22   An inexpensive hand drill stand makes a good shaping and smoothing center for using drum sanding accessories if a drill press is not available.

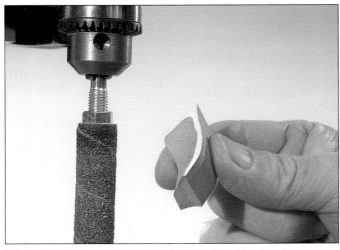

Photo No. 3-23   Drum sanders are ideal for forming convex surfaces.

Photo No. 3-24   An oscillating drum sander is a luxury, not a necessity, that provides fast and cool stock removal with a variety of interchangeable drum sizes.

3. Shape the segments using small routers. Use a small trim router to round-over segmented edges quickly and uniformly. See Photos No. 3-25 and No. 3-26 below and on page 22. Use bits from a ⅛" to a ⅜" radius. See Photos No. 3-27 through No. 3-29 on page 22. Use the pattern for making your own zero-clearance router base. See Drawing No. 3-3 on page 22 and Photos No. 3-30 through No. 3-32 on page 23.

Photo No. 3-25   Various trim routers set up for small segment rounding are: left, two models of Porter-Cable trim routers and right, a Ryobi. Note the auxiliary plastic bases.

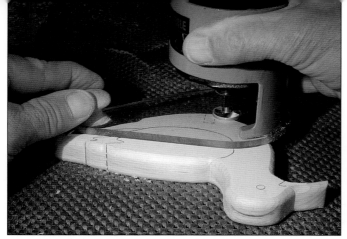

Photo No. 3-26   Round-over on a nonslip router pad. Here, all the outside edges of this profile are rounded-over before the smaller integral segments are cut free into smaller, separate, segments. Then the smaller segments are rounded-over by hand.

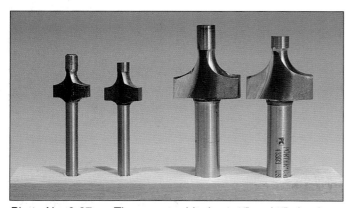

Photo No. 3-27   These router bits have ⅛" and ¼" shanks. The smaller bits are used in high-speed rotary tools, such as a Dremel. Note that the pilots of some bits are ground shorter to allow for routing thinner materials.

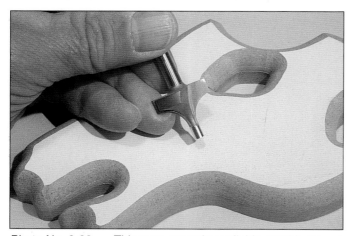

Photo No. 3-28   This new, recently available carbide-tipped router bit has a small brass pilot that is only ⁵⁄₃₂"-diameter. This bit is perfect for getting into tight corners and cuts the MDF unicorn head shown here without dulling.

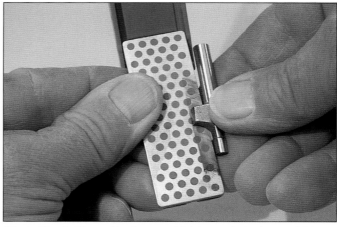

Photo No. 3-29   To sharpen high-speed steel or carbide-tipped bits, use a diamond hone. Work the bit back and forth uniformly on each wing, honing with the same number of strokes. Hone only on the flat, chip sides of the bit.

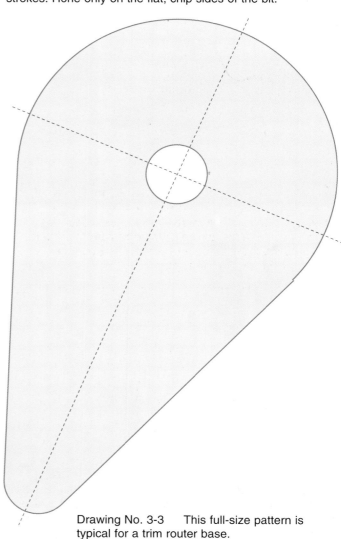

Drawing No. 3-3   This full-size pattern is typical for a trim router base.

Photo No. 3-30   Round-over a medium- to small-sized segment with a small trim router. Note the special shop-made, clear plastic base. Pressure is maintained downward during the cut, forcing the work piece tightly against the non-slip router pad. Perform this operation with caution. Wear suitable eye and hearing protection.

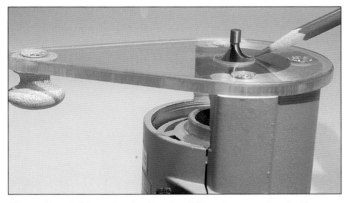

Photo No. 3-31   Look closely at the shop-made plastic router base. Note that the hole for the bit has almost zero-clearance around it, which is essential to support the router when rounding over small segments.

Photo No. 3-32   A small Dremel rotary tool also equipped with a near zero-clearance plastic base for use with a small round-over bit.

4. Apply texture to the segments. Use a wood-burning tool for texturing and quickly producing v-cut lines into surfaces to simulate detail, such as hair. Produce other textured surfaces that might be more difficult to create with files or carving knives. See Photo No. 3-33.

Photo No. 3-33   A wood-burning tool is ideal for adding definition lines to accent various surfaces of individual segments.

5. Reduce the segment thickness. Sometimes it is recommended that certain segments be reduced in thickness. See Photo No. 3-10 on page 18. This task can be done in various ways, but sawing and abrasive cutting are the two easiest options. See Photos No. 3-34 through No. 3-37 below and on page 24.

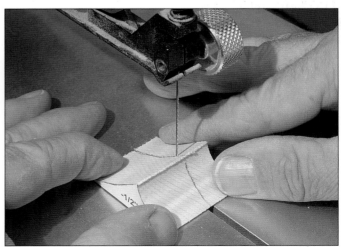

Photo No. 3-34   Small segments can be cut to desired thicknesses with the scroll saw.

23

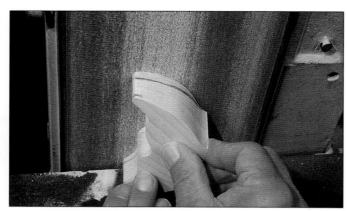

Photo No. 3-35   To taper two sides of a segment, use a 6" vertical belt sanding machine.

Photo No. 3-36 1" vertical belt sanders will handle a variety of wood-shaping jobs, including convex shaping.

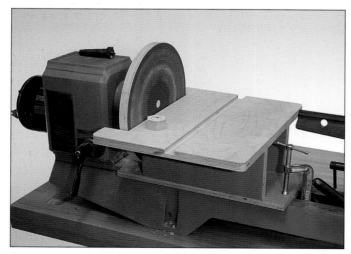

Photo No. 3-37   A disc sander accessory made from plywood for the lathe will do many of the same jobs as belt sanding machines.

24

Use the flat surfaces of belt sanders or disk sanders with coarse abrasives, 36 to 50 or 60 grit, for quick flat, parallel, or tapered-thickness stock removal. Reduce thickness by removing material from the face, or front surface, of the segment. Removing stock from the surface that will be glued to the backer is not a good practice. If you should inadvertently remove material unevenly, or taper the surface, the edges will not fit as tightly as they should to the adjoining segments. Where thickness reduction is required, it will be indicated on the project pattern with a minus (-) sign.

6. Shim selected segments. Glue a shim to the back side of certain inside segments to slightly raise the segments. See Drawing No. 3-4 and accompanying photo. This technique adds to the relief. A segment representing a nose, for example, can make a face appear more realistic if raised just ⅛" above the surrounding segments. Where a shim is required, it will be indicated on the project pattern with a plus (+) sign.

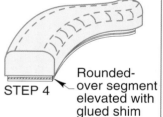

STEP 4   Rounded-over segment elevated with glued shim

Drawing No. 3-4   Certain segments look more realistic when raised in relief. This is accomplished by gluing a small plywood shim under the segment(s).

7. Smooth the segments using scroll sanders. Use scroll sanders, available in several grit sizes, with the scroll saw to smooth segments that have already been shaped. See Photos No. 3-38 and No. 3-39 on the opposite page. Scroll sanders also work well to soften sharp edges or where little wood removal is required. Emery boards (fingernail files) are also useful in the shop. Use them to make your own scroll sanders as shown in Photo No. 3-40 on the opposite page.

8. Smooth the segments using pneumatic and soft drum sanders. Use pneumatic and soft drum sanders

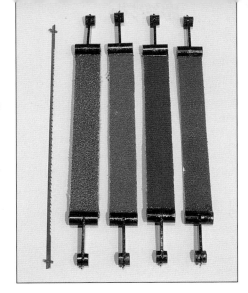

Photo No. 3-38 Scroll sanders are abrasive strips shown here next to a regular pin-type scroll saw blade.

for shaping segmentation and intarsia projects. See Photos No. 3-41 and No. 3-42. The pneumatic drums have the advantage of being inflated to the desired pressure to match the work piece being sanded. The pneumatic type, available from Woodcraft, measures 3" in diameter x 8" in length and can be mounted in a lathe or in a drill press. The less expensive "Flex Drum" sander, manufactured by Seyco Sales Co., attaches to a 1725 rpm motor shaft or to a drill press. The foam-supported abrasive of the flex drum sander is not adjustable as far as hardness is concerned, but it is designed with a medium pliability intended specifically for intarsia work.

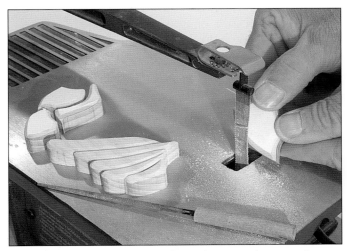

Photo No. 3-39   Use a scroll sander to produce small chamfered edges on ash segments.

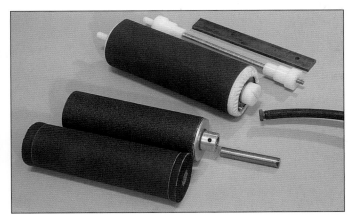

Photo No. 3-41   A pneumatic (air filled) drum sander rotates between the centers of a lathe or can be driven vertically in a drill press (top). An ordinary bicycle tire pump provides the air. A less expensive foam-cushioned sander is designed specifically for contour sanding of segmented and intarsia pieces (bottom).

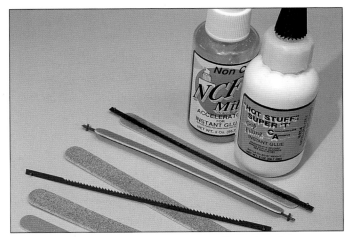

Photo No. 3-40   Make your own scroll sanders from emery boards (fingernail files). If necessary, cut them to length and use super glue or epoxy to adhere them onto used or dull scroll saw blades.

Photo No. 3-42   The foam-cushioned sander is designed to mount onto a ½" or ⅝" motor shaft. It can also be installed in the drill press.

9. Smooth the segments using orbital sanders and flutter wheels. Smooth the segments, using a powered device, such as a small orbital hand-held sander. See Photo No. 3-43. Use flutter abrasive wheels of 150 or 180 grit for smoothing all kinds of contour surfaces. See Photos No. 3-44 and No. 3-45. These drill accessories allow sanding of small segments without injury to your fingers should you get them too close.

Photo No. 3-45 A versatile multiposition drill stand that will clamp to a workbench or a sawhorse is useful to make various sanding and smoothing work stations. Note the tape used to secure the variable-speed trigger switch at the optimum flutter wheel speed, which is about 700 to 1000 RPM.

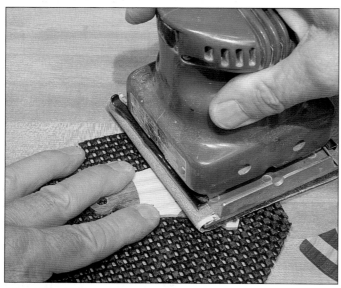

Photo No. 3-43   Small hand-held electric sanders work well for sanding flat and convex surfaces.

Photo No. 3-44   Flutter wheels of 150 and 180 grit will smooth most any surface contour.

IV. Color & Finish the Segments.

Once the segments are shaped and smoothed, finish the individual segments as desired.

Use oil stains, natural finishes, opaque colored paints, or transparent colored dyes and colored stains. To assure a good glue bond, do not finish concealed gluing areas along the edges or the backs of segments. See Photo No. 3-46.

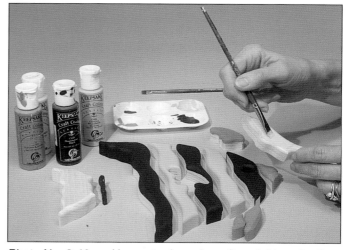

Photo No. 3-46   Use water-based acrylic paint to color the individual shaped segments. Note that all of the nonvisible gluing surfaces at the edges are left unpainted to insure a good glue bond.

Transparent colors are very effective and yield interesting results as they do not conceal the wood's figure, or grain. See Photos No. 3-47 and No. 3-48.

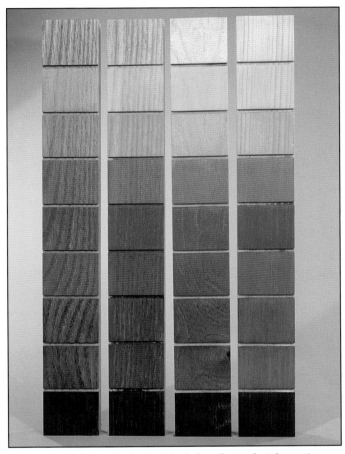

Photo No. 3-47   Natural, light-colored woods take water-based wood dye colors best. Woods, left to right: oak, ash, birch, and pine.

Photo No. 3-48   Concentrated water-based dyes are commonly used to color wood.

When using water-based dyes, first sponge-dampen the surfaces. Allow to dry. Sand the surfaces with the grain to remove the raised grain. Then moisten the wood and wipe out with the grain again just before the dye is applied. Create lighter shades by diluting the dye pigment with water. Watered-down acrylic paints also can be used to suggest color, yet still allow the wood grain to show through.

An oil-based, colored stain product is available that is much easier to apply than water-based dyes. See Photo No. 3-49. It is a tung oil finish with pigments that imitate a dye. To use this product, simply wipe it on the dry, sanded wood with paper towels.

Photo No. 3-49   Colored stains are easy-to-use (but more expensive) products that are applied to dry, raw wood with paper towels.

Always test whatever finish you choose for any project on scrap material first to assure that it will deliver the look that you want before applying it to your project.

V. Assemble the Segments.
1. Place the remaining pattern photocopy on a clean, flat surface. Then cover it with waxed paper or freezer paper that is fairly transparent. You can also use a plastic wrap. See Photo No. 3-50 on page 28.

Glue the segments together at the edges, using the adhesive of your choice. Yellow carpenter's glue and instant/super glues are recommended because they set fairly quickly.

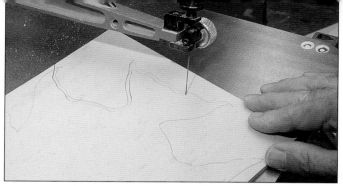

Photo No. 3-52   With the saw table tilted 15˚ to 20˚, cut ⅛"
inside the layout line to make the backer.

3. Glue the backer to the assembled segments. See
Photo No. 3-53.

Photo No. 3-53   Use spring clamps or weights to hold the
backer to the preglued segments. Notice the tenon shown at
the pencil point which will fit into a base, making this particular project free-standing.

4. Attach a sawtooth picture hanger to projects that
are to be hung on the wall. See Photo No. 3-54.

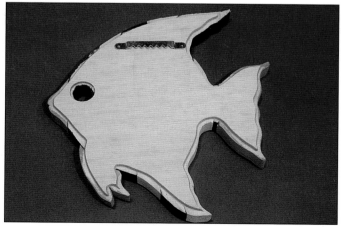

Photo No. 3-54   This rear view shows the plywood backer
and a sawtooth picture hanger, which is typical of all wall-
hanging segmentation pieces.

Photo No. 3-50   Reassemble the segments and glue them
together at the edges to make the whole again.

VI. Make a Backer.

1. Carefully lay the assembled segments onto a piece
of ⅛"- to ¼"-thick plywood and trace the outline
shape of the project. See Photo No. 3-51.

Photo No. 3-51   For one-sided, wall-hanging projects,
trace around the assembly onto a ⅛"- or ¼"-thick plywood
backer.

2. Cut a backer piece from the plywood. See Photo
No. 3-52.

Chapter 4
Segmented Fish

Segmented fish make colorful, decorative accents for every home. Here are three different designs, all easy to make.

Striped Fish

This fish design is made to hang on the wall. It is constructed from a thinner material with a plywood backer.

Supplies
¾"-thick pine: 8" x 9¼"
⅛"- to ¼"-thick plywood: 8" x 9¼"
Basic Tools & Supplies from page 15

Instructions
See Segmentation Technique Instructions on pages 16–28.

I. Prepare the Patterns.
1. Apply one Striped Fish pattern from page 30 to plywood.

II. Cut the Wood.

III. Shape & Smooth the Wood.

IV. Color & Finish the Segments.

V. Assemble the Segments.

VI. Make a Backer.

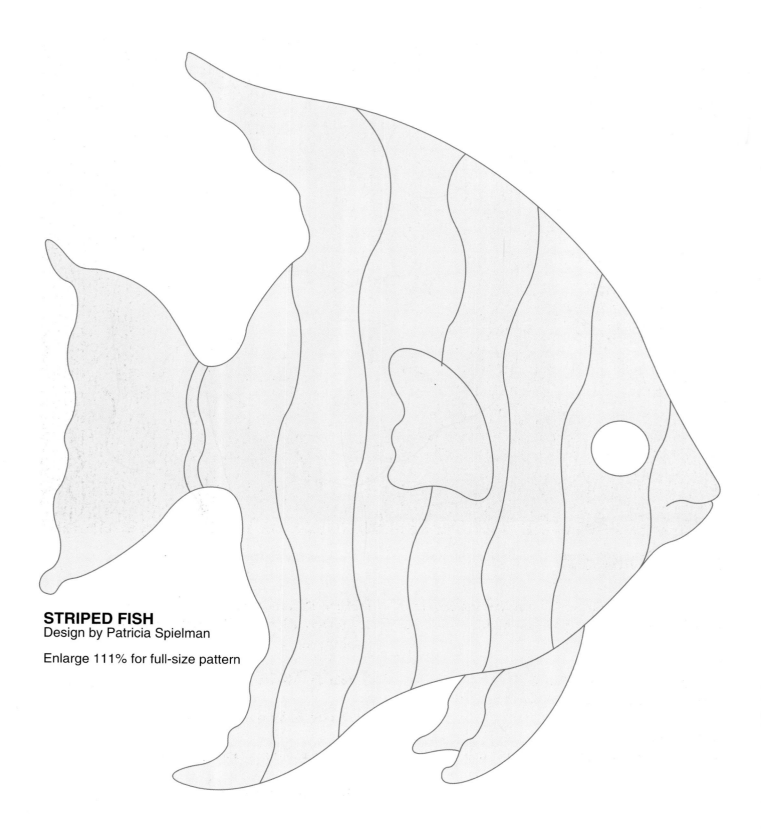

STRIPED FISH
Design by Patricia Spielman

Enlarge 111% for full-size pattern

Pink & Blue Fish

This fish design is made of thicker material to stand by itself without a plywood backer.

Supplies
1⅛"- to 1½"-thick pine: 7" x 10"
Basic Tools & Supplies from page 15

Instructions
See Segmentation Technique Instructions on pages 16–28.

I. Prepare the Patterns.
1. Apply one Pink & Blue Fish pattern from page 32 to plywood.

II. Cut the Wood.

III. Shape & Smooth the Wood.

IV. Color & Finish the Segments.

V. Assemble the Segments.

PINK & BLUE FISH
Design by Patricia Spielman

Enlarge 111% for full-size pattern

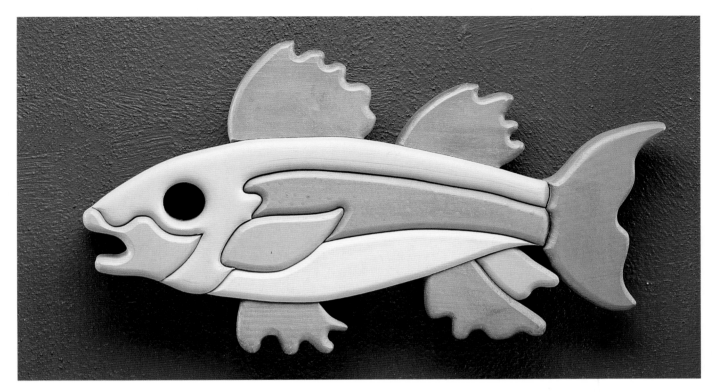

Speckled Fish

Supplies
1⅛"- to 1½"-thick pine: 6¼" x 11"
Basic Tools & Supplies from page 15

Instructions
See Segmentation Technique Instructions on pages 16–28.

I. Prepare the Patterns.
1. Apply one Speckled Fish pattern from page 34 to pine.

II. Cut the Wood.

III. Shape & Smooth the Wood.
1. Using a pencil, draw guidelines for stock removal. Reduce the stock thickness on a belt sander. See Photos No. 4-1 and 4-2.

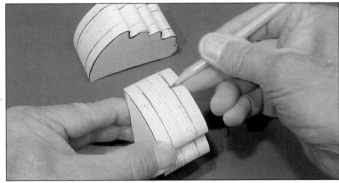

Photo No. 4-1   Finger-gauge the material to be removed from the upper fins to reduce their thickness.

Photo No. 4-2   Sand the tapered tail segment of Speckled Fish design on a belt sander.

33

IV. Color & Finish the Segments.

V. Assemble the Segments.

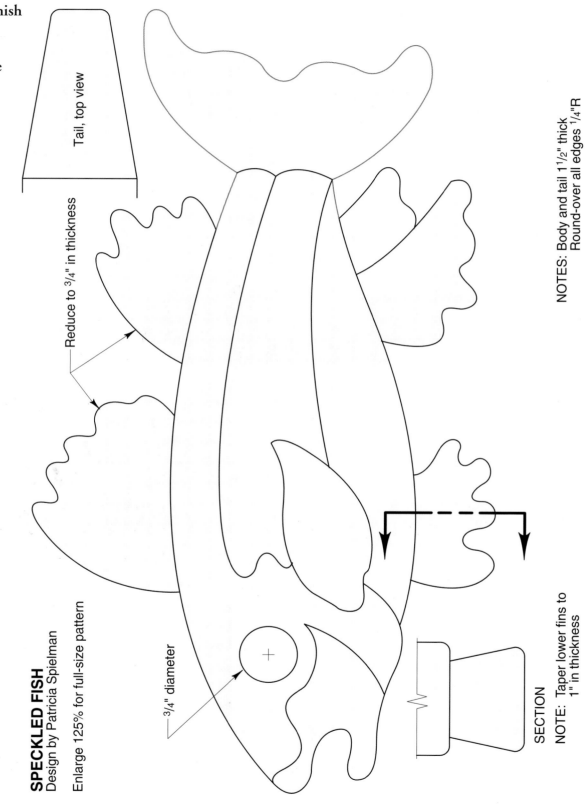

Tail, top view

Reduce to 3/4" in thickness

SPECKLED FISH
Design by Patricia Spielman

Enlarge 125% for full-size pattern

3/4" diameter

SECTION

NOTE: Taper lower fins to 1" in thickness

NOTES: Body and tail 1 1/2" thick
Round-over all edges 1/4"R

Chapter 5
Segmented Birds

Two-piece Shore Bird

Segmentation does not get any easier than this project made from scrap plywood.

Supplies
⅜"-thick Baltic birch plywood: 3" x 7"
⅝"-thick pine: 2¼" x 2¼"
³⁄₁₆" dowel: 5½" long
Basic Tools & Supplies from page 15

Instructions
See Segmentation Technique Instructions on pages 16–28.

I. Prepare the Patterns.
1. Apply one Two-piece Shore Bird pattern from page 36 to Baltic birch plywood.

II. Cut the Wood.
1. Cut out the outside profile of the bird.

2. Drill a ³⁄₁₆" hole ½" deep in the bottom segment of the bird for the dowel.

3. Cut out the segments. See Photo No. 5-1.

4. Cut out the base from pine.

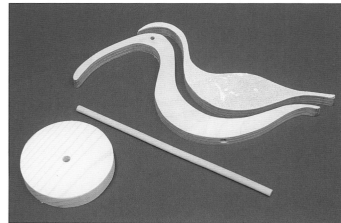

Photo No. 5-1   The Two-piece Shore Bird is shown with the segments and parts cut out.

III. Shape & Smooth the Wood.

1. Slightly chamfer the edges along the glue line between the two segments. See Photo No. 5-2.

2. Drill the eye hole and a hole through the center of the base.

IV. Color & Finish the Segments.

V. Assemble the Segments.

1. Apply wood glue to both ends of the dowel. Insert the dowel into the base and bottom segment.

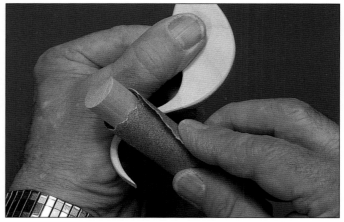

Photo No. 5-2   Use 80-grit abrasive over a dowel to chamfer the edges along the glue joint.

TWO-PIECE SHORE BIRD
Design by Patricia Spielman

Full-size pattern

Base ⅝" thick

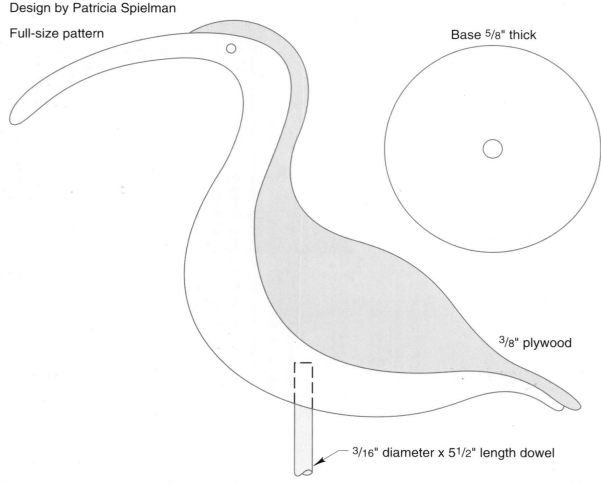

3/8" plywood

3/16" diameter x 5½" length dowel

Four-piece Sea Gull

Here's another quick and easy project that is made similar to the Two-piece Shore Bird.

Supplies
¾"-thick clear pine: 4" x 7¼"
¾"-thick pine: 2" x 3"
³⁄₁₆" dowel: 5½" long
Basic Tools & Supplies from page 15

Instructions
See Segmentation Technique Instructions on pages 16–28.

I. Prepare the Patterns.
1. Apply one Four-piece Sea Gull pattern from page 38 to clear pine.

II. Cut the Wood.
1. Cut out the outside profile of the bird.

2. Make two cuts along the bill, partway in from the outside, but do not cut the bill free—leave about ⅛" of the line uncut. See Photo No. 5-3.

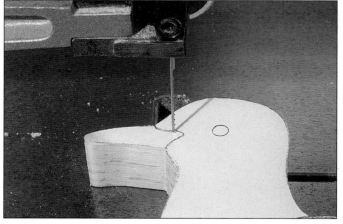

Photo No. 5-3   Do not cut the bill free until after rounding over the entire outside profile. Here, one cut is made partway inward from the outside edge before rounding over.

III. Shape & Smooth the Wood.
1. Round-over the entire outside profile (including the bill) on the front and the back to a ³⁄₁₆" radius.

2. Drill a ¼" hole about ½" deep in the bottom of the bird for the dowel. See Photos No. 5-4 and No. 5-5.

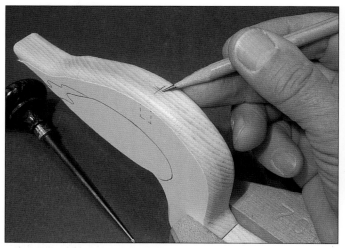

Photo No. 5-4   Here, all the outside edges have been rounded over with a ³⁄₁₆" radius router bit and the edge is marked for the dowel hole. Finger-gauge from each surface to quickly produce two marks at the approximate center. Drill at the center between these marks.

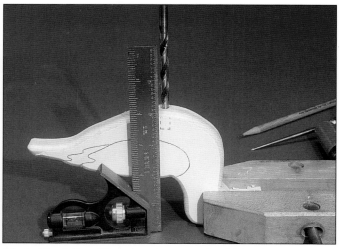

Photo No. 5-5   The piece is set up for drilling into the edge.

II. Cut the Wood.

1. Cut out the segments, including the remainder of the bill.

2. Cut the base from the ⅝"-thick pine.

III. Shape & Smooth the Wood.

1. Drill the eye hole and a hole through the center of the base.

IV. Color & Finish the Segments.

V. Assemble the Segments.

1. Apply wood glue to both ends of the dowel. Insert the dowel into the base and the bottom of the bird.

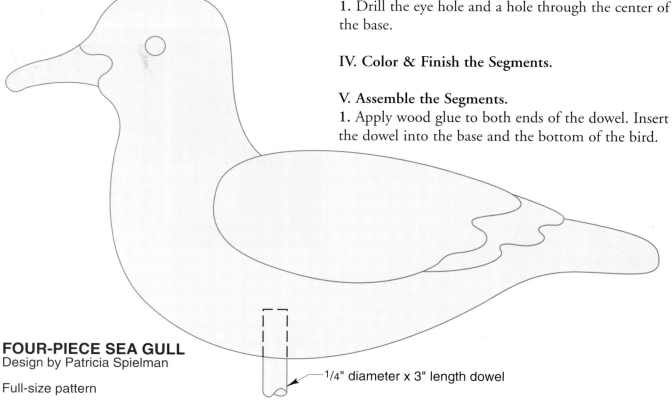

FOUR-PIECE SEA GULL
Design by Patricia Spielman

Full-size pattern

—1/4" diameter x 3" length dowel

Carved Duck

The photo shows a dimensionally contoured decoy. This makes for an excellent decorative accent for those who love the outdoors.

Supplies
1⅛"- to 1½"-thick pine: 5" x 10"
Basic Tools & Supplies from page 15

Instructions
See Segmentation Technique Instructions on pages 16–28.

I. Prepare the Patterns.
1. Apply one Carved Duck pattern from page 40 to pine.

II. Cut the Wood.

III. Shape & Smooth the Wood.
1. To carve a more realistic head and bill , use a center, pencil guideline drawn along the edges. This will help you keep the shape(s) symmetrical as you form it. See Photo No. 5-6.

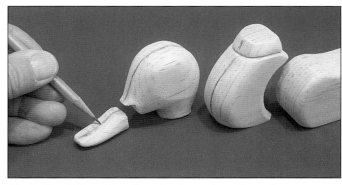

Photo No. 5-6   Pencil center lines along the edges as shown to help keep the shapes symmetrical if carving a more realistic head.

IV. Color & Finish the Segments.
1. Coat some segments with a clear, natural finish and color others with acrylic paint before gluing them together.

V. Assemble the Segments.

CARVED DUCK
Design by
Patricia Spielman

Full-size pattern

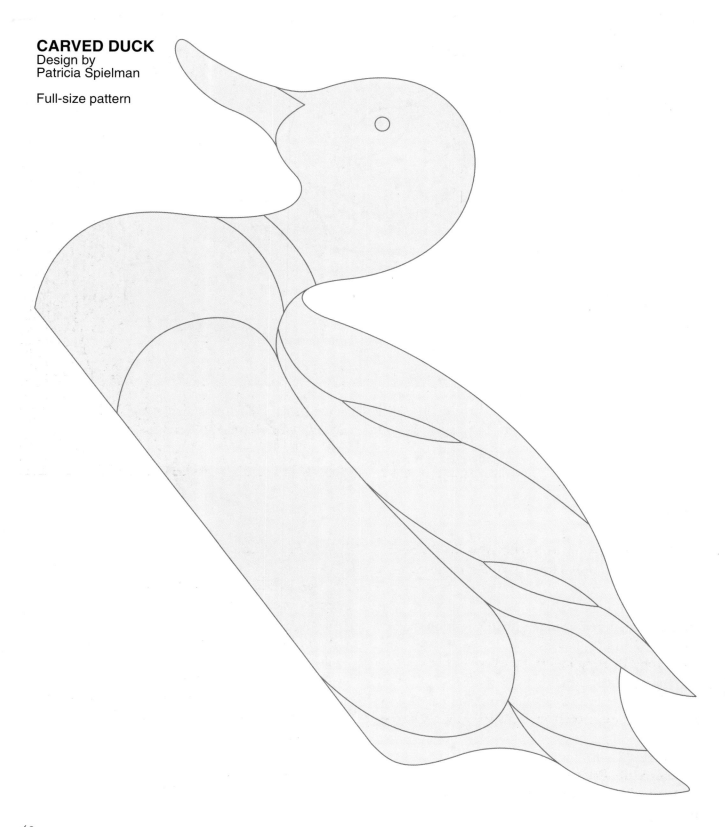

Duck Decoy

This pleasantly formed figure of a duck would look wonderful on the mantle of the fireplace in the study.

Supplies
1⅛"- to 1½"-thick pine: 5" x 11"
Basic Tools & Supplies from page 15

Instructions
See Segmentation Technique Instructions on pages 16–28.

I. Prepare the Patterns.
1. Apply one Duck Decoy pattern from page 42 to pine.

II. Cut the Wood.

III. Shape & Smooth the Wood.
1. Shape the head as desired.

2. Round-over or chamfer all remaining segments.

IV. Color & Finish the Segments.
1. Coat some segments with a clear, natural finish and color others with acrylic paint before gluing them together.

V. Assemble the Segments.

DUCK DECOY
Design by Patricia Spielman

Enlarge 105% for full-size pattern

Chapter 5
Segmented Birds

Two-piece Shore Bird

Segmentation does not get any easier than this project made from scrap plywood.

Supplies
⅜"-thick Baltic birch plywood: 3" x 7"
⅝"-thick pine: 2¼" x 2¼"
³⁄₁₆" dowel: 5½" long
Basic Tools & Supplies from page 15

Instructions
See Segmentation Technique Instructions on
pages 16–28.

I. Prepare the Patterns.
1. Apply one Two-piece Shore Bird pattern from page 36 to Baltic birch plywood.

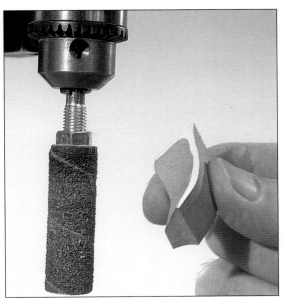

Photo No. 5-1   The Two-piece Shore Bird is shown with the segments and parts cut out.

Photo No. 5-2   Use 80-grit abrasive over a dowel to chamfer the edges along the glue joint.

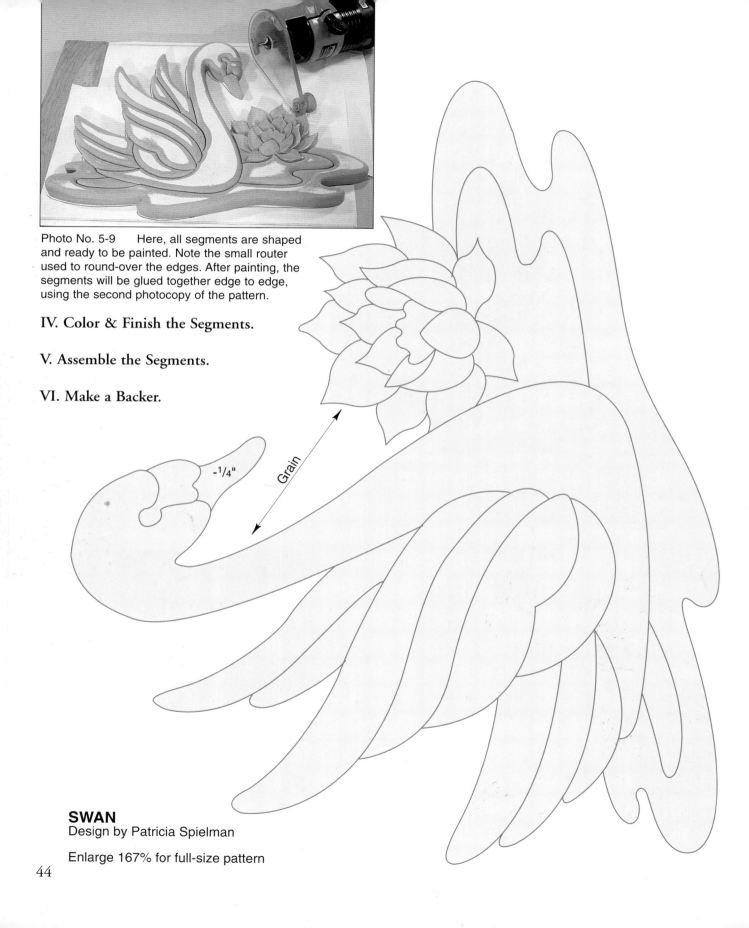

Photo No. 5-9   Here, all segments are shaped and ready to be painted. Note the small router used to round-over the edges. After painting, the segments will be glued together edge to edge, using the second photocopy of the pattern.

IV. Color & Finish the Segments.

V. Assemble the Segments.

VI. Make a Backer.

-¹/₄"

Grain

SWAN
Design by Patricia Spielman

Enlarge 167% for full-size pattern

44

Road Runner

Noted for its remarkable running speed, this bird from the great Southwest is known and adored everywhere. Make the bird with or without the desert scene background and frame.

Supplies

¾"-thick clear pine: 5" x 12" for the body and front leg

⅜"-thick clear pine: 1" x 3¼" for the rear leg

⅛"-thick Baltic Birch plywood: 1" x 2¼" for cactus segment

¼"-thick Baltic Birch plywood: 3½" x 6½" for cactus segments

⅛"-thick Baltic Birch plywood: 9⅞" x 17¼" for horizon strips

¼"-thick Baltic Birch plywood: 9¼" x 17¼" for backer

¾"-thick straight grain oak or ash: 1⅛" x 60" for frame

Basic Tools & Supplies from page 15

Instructions

See Segmentation Technique Instructions on pages 16–28.

I. Prepare the Patterns.

1. Apply one Road Runner pattern from pages 47–48 to oak and Baltic birch plywood.

II. Cut the Wood.

1. Cut the strips from the 9½" x 17¼" piece of plywood on the table saw (or scroll saw and band saw).

III. Shape & Smooth the Wood.

1. Chamfer the plywood strips.

2. Reduce stock thickness of segments as indicated on the pattern. Reduce the three segments of the "bushy" crest to ⅜". Texture these segments with a wood-burning tool or file. See Photo No. 5-10.

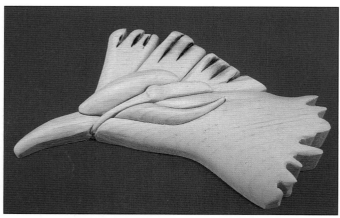

Photo No. 5-10   A wood-burning tool or file is used to cut grooves in the bushy crest.

IV. Color & Finish the Segments.

1. Create the texture on the upper body using a stippling action of the paintbrush. See Photo No. 5-11.

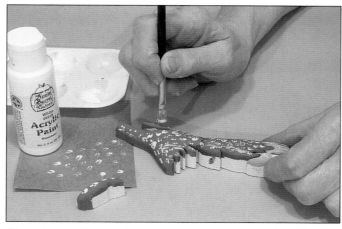

Photo No. 5-11   A stippling action creates a textured look on the body.

V. Assemble the Segments. & VI. Make a Backer.

1. Glue the ⅛" plywood strips to a piece of plywood backer material that measures ¼" x 9¼" x 17¼".

2. Glue the Road Runner and cacti onto the painted strips.

VII. Make the Frame

1. Prepare the frame stock using a table saw and jointer. Cut the pieces to rough length. See the frame section detail below.

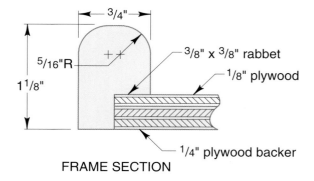

FRAME SECTION

2. Cut or rout a ⅜" x ⅜" rabbet along the inside back edges. Round-over the front edges using the router table. See Photo No. 5-12.

Photo No. 5-12   Here, frame stock is rounded over on the router table.

3. Miter the corners, sand, assemble, and finish with a penetrating Danish oil finish.

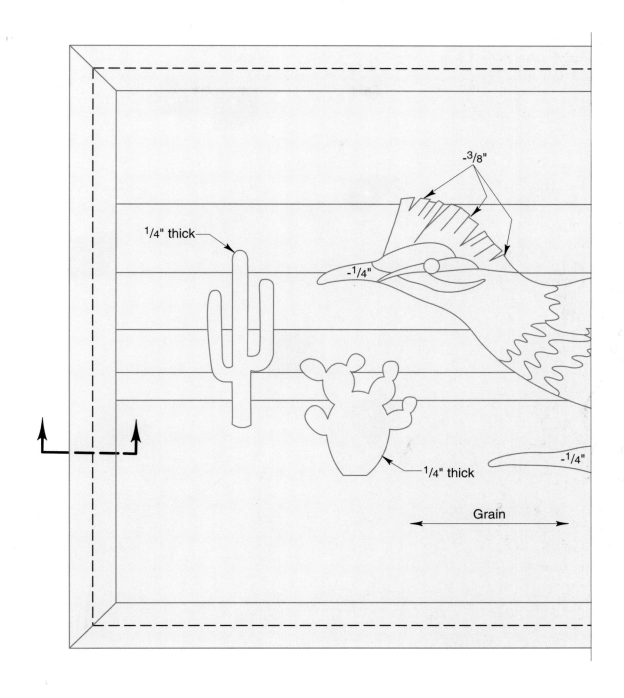

ROAD RUNNER
Design by Patricia Spielman

Enlarge 153% for full-size pattern

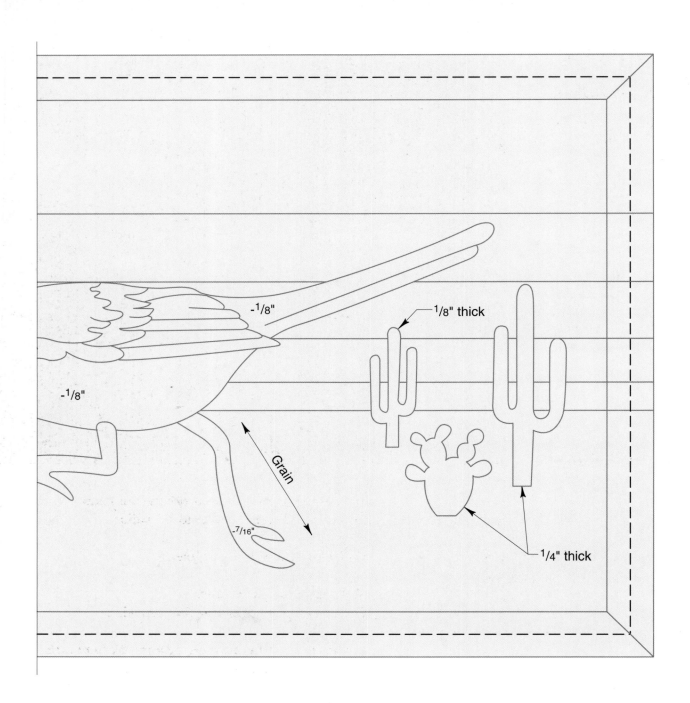

ROAD RUNNER
Design by Patricia Spielman

Enlarge 153% for full-size pattern

Chapter 6
Halloween &
Thanksgiving

Pumpkin & Ghost

Supplies
¾"-thick MDF: 8½" x 9¾" for pumpkin; 6½" x 11½"
   for ghost
⅛"-thick plywood: 8½" x 9¾" for pumpkin backer
Basic Tools & Supplies from page 15

Instructions
See Segmentation Technique Instructions on pages
16–28.

I. Prepare the Patterns.
1. Apply one Pumpkin & Ghost pattern from page
50 to MDF.

II. Cut the Wood.

III. Shape & Smooth the Wood.
1. Reduce the stem and leaf segments to ½" thickness. Slightly round-over the pumpkin stem, leaf,
and stem segments. Round-over the pumpkin
segments and ghost profiles to ⁵⁄₁₆" radius.

IV. Color & Finish the Segments.

V. Assemble the Segments.
1. Coil two pieces of green electrical wire.

2. Drill holes in the stem segment for the wire curls
and glue them in place.

VI. Make a Backer.

Design Tip
   The ghost can be temporarily attached to the
back of the pumpkin with double-sided tape. After
Halloween, it can be removed and the pumpkin can
be used alone as a Thanksgiving decoration.

PUMPKIN & GHOST
Design by Patricia Spielman

Enlarge 142% for full-size pattern

II. Cut the Wood.

III. Shape & Smooth the Wood.

1. Reduce the thickness of those segments indicated with a minus (-) sign on the drawing. Remember, it is best to remove material from the front rather than the back.

2. Cut shims ⅛"- and ¼"-thick to elevate the wing segments marked with a plus (+) on the pattern.

3. Taper the feather segments inward toward the body using a disc or belt sander. **Note:** Not all segments are rounded over, such as the edges of the feathers where they butt to the body. See Photo No. 6-1. These and the edges of thinner segments not rounded over are indicated on the pattern with a small "V" mark.

Holiday Turkey

This Thanksgiving wall plaque involves basic techniques. In addition to reducing the thickness of some segments as indicated on the pattern, the two central wing segments are shimmed and the feathers taper from ¾" in thickness at the tips to ⅜" where they meet the body.

Supplies
¾"-thick MDF: 9¾" x 13"
⅛"- to ¼"-thick plywood: 9¾" x 13"
Basic Tools & Supplies from page 15

Instructions
See Segmentation Technique Instructions on pages 16–28.

I. Prepare the Patterns.
1. Apply one Holiday Turkey pattern from page 52 to MDF.

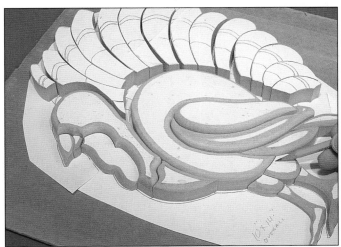

Photo No. 6-1   Not all edges are rounded over, such as these thinner segments that butt to a thicker or shimmed segment.

IV. Color & Finish the Segments.

V. Assemble the Segments.

VI. Make a Backer.

Round-over feather segments
and beak separation
1/16"R

-1/4" -1/4"

-1/4"

+1/4"

+1/8"

-3/8" -1/4"

-1/2" -3/8"

HOLIDAY TURKEY
Design by Patricia Spielman

Enlarge 150% for full-size pattern

NOTE: Round-over all edges 1/4" or 5/16"R
        except those noted:
        < Denotes edges not rounded over
        - Indicates thickness reduction
        + Indicates shim to increase thickness

Chapter 7
Christmas

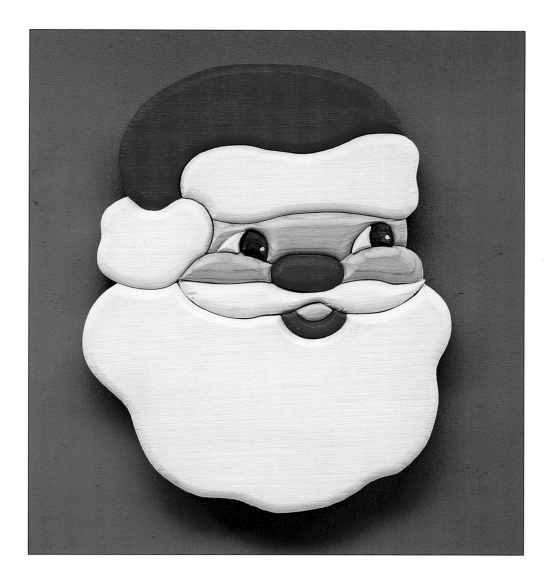

Santa Face

Supplies
¾"-thick pine: 8½" x 6¾"
⅛"- to ¼"-thick plywood: 8½" x 6¾"
Basic Tools & Supplies from page 15

Instructions
See Segmentation Technique Instructions on pages
16–28.

I. Prepare the Patterns.
1. Apply one Santa Face pattern from page 54 to
pine.

II. Cut the Wood.

III. Shape & Smooth the Wood.
1. Round-over all edges ¼" radius.

IV. Color & Finish the Segments.
1. Apply red aniline stain or red acrylic paint to the
cap, nose, and lower mouth segments. Apply a
natural finish to the cheeks and upper mouth. Paint
the right segments on both eyes black. Dot the eyes
with white paint. Apply a whitewash to all other
segments by wiping on a thinned white acrylic paint.

V. Assemble the Segments.

VI. Make a Backer.

SANTA FACE
Design by Patricia Spielman

Enlarge 135% for full-size pattern

Angel

The heavenly holiday angel is made of ash, but almost any other species of wood can also be used. This project is finished so some of the wood figure, or grain, shows through.

Supplies
½"-thick ash: 8¼" x 17½"
⅛"- to ¼"-thick plywood: 8¼" x 17½"
Basic Tools & Supplies from page 15

Instructions
See Segmentation Technique Instructions on pages 16–28.

I. Prepare the Patterns.
1. Apply one Angel pattern from page 56 to ash.

II. Cut the Wood.

III. Shape & Smooth the Wood.
1. Chamfer all edges about ⅟₁₆" to ⅛".

IV. Color & Finish the Segments.
1. Finish each segment with a coat of acrylic paint thinned with water. Paint it on and then wipe it off immediately with a paper towel or cotton rag.

V. Assemble the Segments.
1. Assemble the segments. See Photo No. 7-1.

Photo No. 7-1 Assemble the pre-finished segments, gluing them edge to edge over a second copy of the pattern protected with waxed paper.

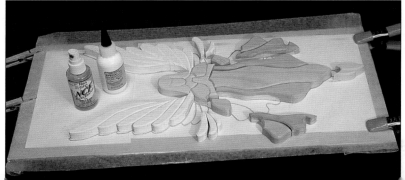

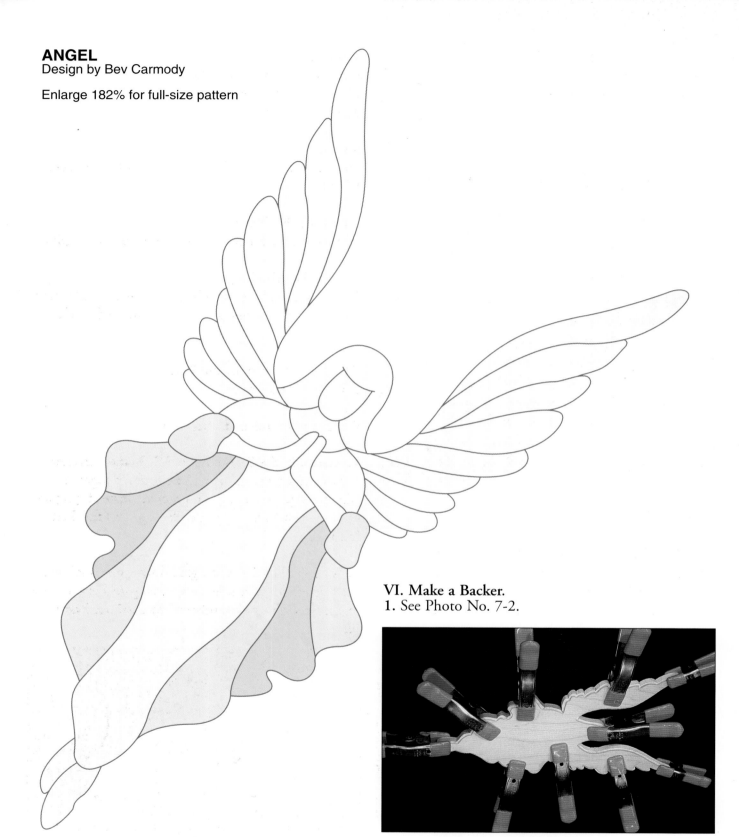

ANGEL
Design by Bev Carmody

Enlarge 182% for full-size pattern

VI. Make a Backer.
1. See Photo No. 7-2.

Photo No. 7-2   Use spring clamps to hold the backer to the preglued segments.

Nativity

This project has an integral frame cut around all the segments. Unless you employ some precautions in assembly, large gaps between segments may result due to an accumulation of space resulting from the many saw kerfs. See Photo No. 7-3.

Supplies
¾"-thick clear ash: 8¾" x 12"
⅛"- to ¼"-thick plywood: 8¾" x 12"
Basic Tools & Supplies from page 15

Instructions
See Segmentation Technique Instructions on pages 16–28.

I. Prepare the Patterns.
1. Apply one Nativity pattern from page 58 to pine.

II. Cut the Wood.
1. Drill small blade-threading holes; one at an inside frame corner and one along the bottom edge of the child's face.

III. Shape & Smooth the Wood.
1. Chamfer the edges.

IV. Color & Finish the Segments.

V. Assemble the Segments. & VI. Make a Backer.
1. Do not attempt to glue the segments together edge to edge as is the usual practice. Instead, prepare the plywood backer and glue the cut and finished frame to it.

2. When the glue has set, glue down the remaining prefinished segments, leaving equal gaps between the segments with small cardboard spacers. See Photo No. 7-4.

Photo No. 7-3   Because of the surrounding frame and many saw kerfs, excessive space may result unless all segments are spaced evenly.

Photo No. 7-4   Small pieces of cardboard are inserted between all segments. Space them uniformly as they are glued to a plywood backer.

NATIVITY
Design by Patricia Spielman

Enlarge 142% for full-size pattern

Madonna & Child

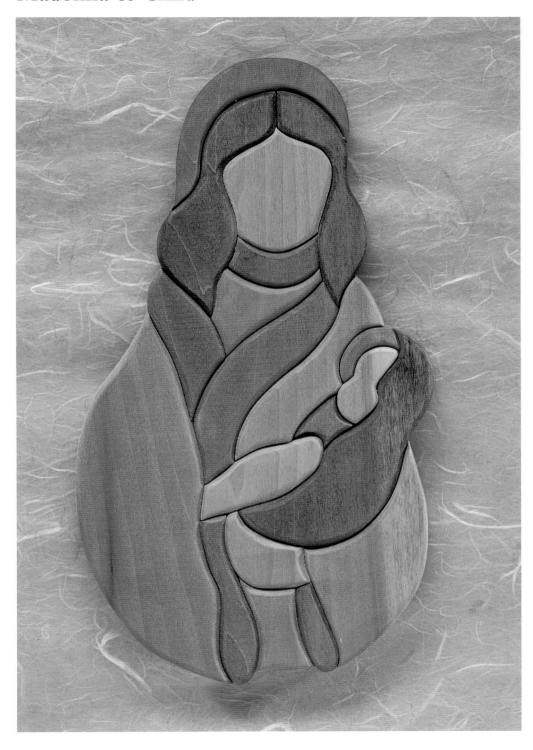

This project is made from poplar with various segments colored with oil stains.

Supplies
¾"-thick poplar: 7¼" x 13"
⅛"- to ¼"-thick plywood:
   7¼" x 13¼"
Basic Tools & Supplies
   from page 15

Instructions
See Segmentation Technique Instructions on pages 16–28.

I. Prepare the Patterns.
1. Apply one Madonna & Child pattern from page 60 to poplar.

II. Cut the Wood.

III. Shape & Smooth the Wood.
1. Chamfer all the edges.

IV. Color & Finish the Segments.
1. Coat the entire project with one or more coats of a nongloss clear finish.

V. Assemble the Segments.

VI. Make a Backer.

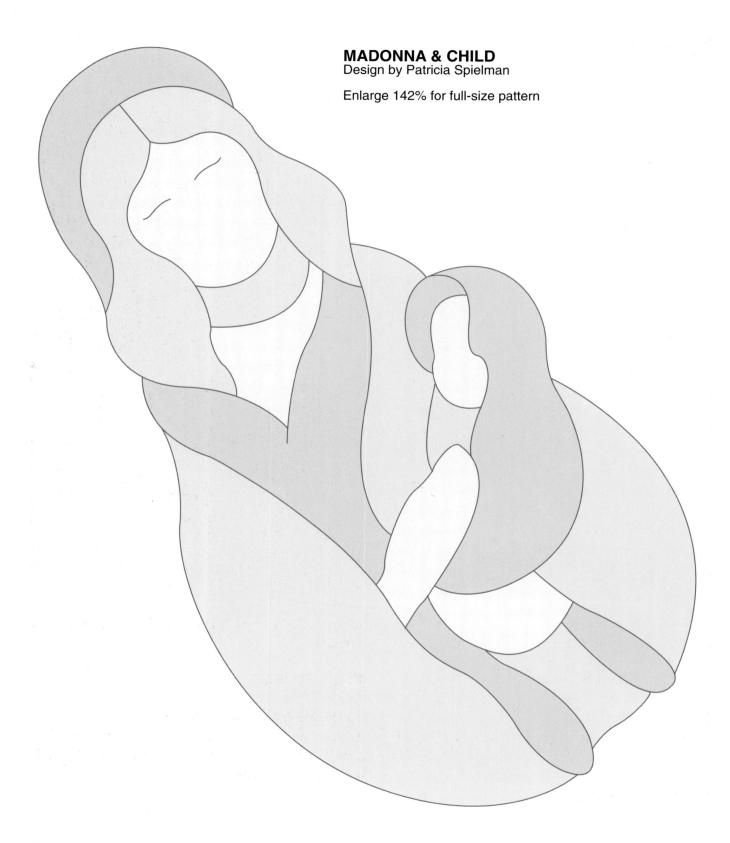

MADONNA & CHILD
Design by Patricia Spielman

Enlarge 142% for full-size pattern

Chapter 8
Fantasy

Made of natural-finished butternut, two of these charming pieces of wall art have the look of fine carvings. Select clear, straight-grained wood of any suitable species that has some figure, or grain, pattern to it. Pine, redwood, walnut, and mahogany are also all good choices.

Sun Face

Supplies
¾"-thick butternut: 8" x 8"
⅛"- to ¼"-thick plywood: 8" x 8"
Basic Tools & Supplies from page 15

Instructions
See Segmentation Technique Instructions on pages 16–28.

I. Prepare the Patterns.
1. Apply one Sun Face pattern from page 63 to butternut. Mount the pattern so the wood grain runs vertically.

II. Cut the Wood.

III. Shape & Smooth the Wood.
1. Reduce the thickness of those segments marked with a minus (-) on the patterns. See Photos No. 8-1 and No. 8-2 on page 62.

61

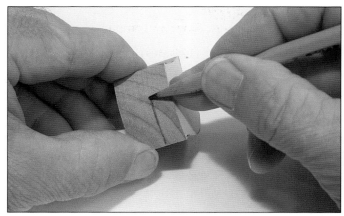

Photo No. 8-1   Finger-gauge a guide line for reducing the thickness. Notice that the paper pattern is still attached to the facing surface of the wood. Always remove stock from face surfaces, not the backs.

Photo No. 8-2   The perimeter segments of the Sun Face have been reduced in thickness. Not all edges of all segments are rounded over. Here, a pencil mark indicates where the rounding over of a higher adjacent segment should begin.

2. Carefully work those segments with short vertical grain, especially the upper lip of the Sun Face. See Photo No. 8-3. Use a coarse-grit drum sander with light pressure to remove stock quickly without fracturing the delicate tips. See Photo No. 8-4.

Photo No. 8-3
The upper lip of
Sun Face has
"short grain," which
must be worked
very carefully so it
does not fracture.

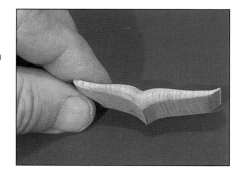

Photo No. 8-4   A small, high-speed rotary tool, fitted with a coarse-grit drum sander, makes edge rounding easy.

3. Make shims for the cheeks, nose, eye brows, and chin of the Sun Face.

4. Sand all segments carefully, removing all cross-grain scratches resulting from coarse abrasives.

IV. Color & Finish the Segments.
1. Paint the eye segments white with black. See the photo on page 61.

V. Assemble the Segments.
1. Apply a clear, nongloss finish.

VI. Make a Backer.
1. See Photo No. 8-5.

Photo No. 8-5   After the segments have been glued back together at the edges, trace the outline on ⅛" or ¼" plywood backer material.

SUN FACE
Design by R. Stephan Toman

Enlarge 111% for full-size pattern

NOTE: Make each eye as one piece and paint on details

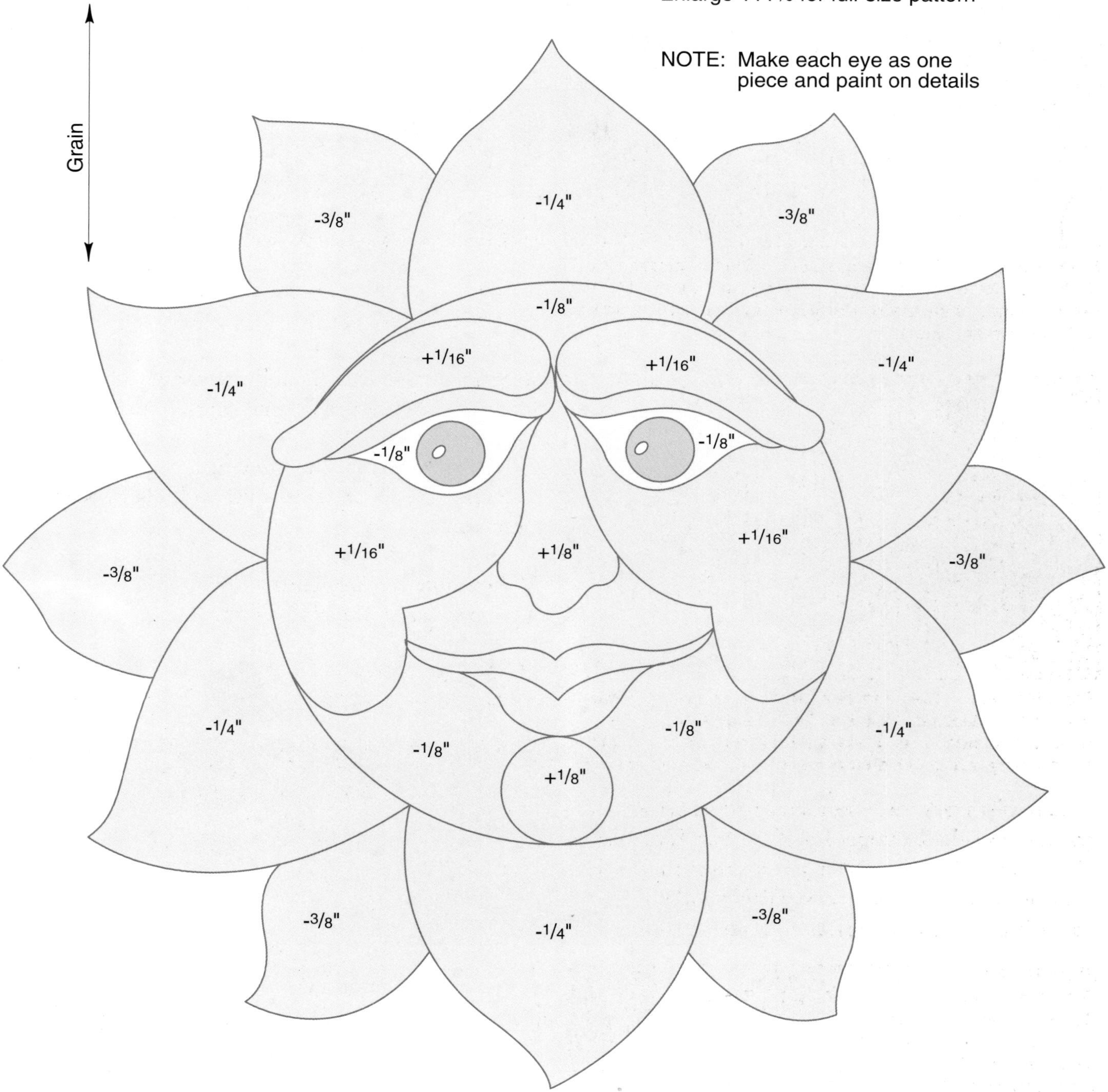

Grain

-3/8"

-1/4"

-3/8"

-1/8"

+1/16"

+1/16"

-1/4"

-1/4"

-1/8"

-1/8"

-1/8"

-3/8"

+1/16"

+1/8"

+1/16"

-3/8"

-1/4"

-1/8"

-1/8"

-1/4"

+1/8"

-3/8"

-1/4"

-3/8"

Moon Face

Supplies
¾"-thick butternut 8" x 8"
⅛"- to ¼"-thick plywood: 8" x 8"
Basic Tools & Supplies from page 15

Instructions
See Segmentation Technique Instructions on pages 16–28.

I. Prepare the Patterns.
1. Apply one Moon Face pattern from page 66 to butternut. Mount the pattern so the wood grain runs vertically.

II. Cut the Wood.

III. Shape & Smooth the Wood.

1. Reduce the thickness of those segments marked with a minus (-) on the patterns.

2. Carefully work those segments with short vertical grain. Use a coarse-grit drum sander with light pressure to remove stock quickly without fracturing the delicate tips.

3. Make a ⅛" shim for the cheek of the Moon Face. See Photo No. 8-6.

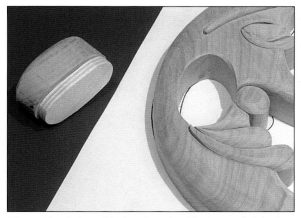

Photo No. 8-6   Notice that the ⅛" plywood shim is glued to the back of the cheek segment.

4. Taper the surface of the Moon Face from the nose toward the cap from ¾" to about ½" in thickness. Taper the cap from ¾" to about ¼" at the juncture of the vertical ribbon segment that will be attached to the star.

5. Sand all segments carefully, removing all cross-grain scratches resulting from coarse abrasives.

IV. Color & Finish the Segments.

V. Assemble the Segments.

1. Assemble all segments, gluing them together edge to edge, except the ribbon and star segments. See Photo No. 8-7.

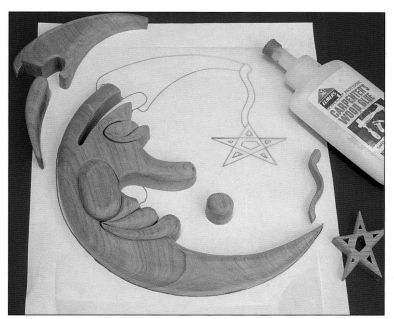

Photo No. 8-7   Glue the cut, shaped, and sanded segments together, edge to edge, over an extra copy of the pattern. Note the waxed paper protecting the pattern.

VI. Make a Backer.

1. Glue the ribbon and star segments on after the backer has been glued in place. See Photo No. 8-8.

2. Apply a clear, nongloss finish.

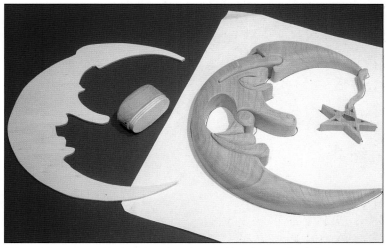

Photo No. 8-8   Notice that the plywood backer at the left does not include backing support for the star or hanging ribbon segments.

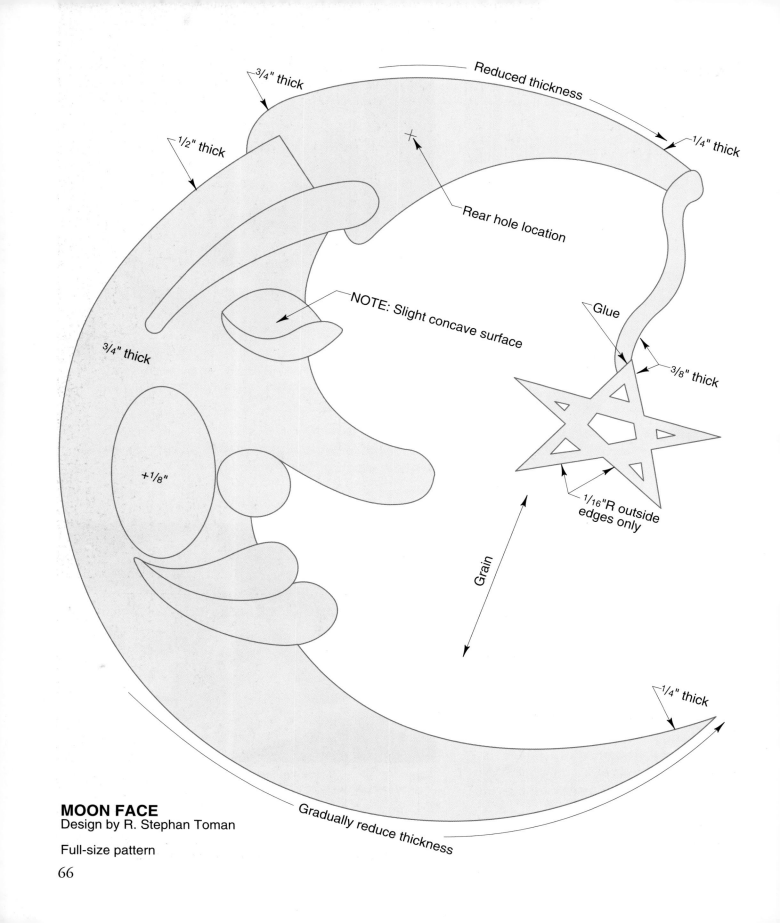

MOON FACE
Design by R. Stephan Toman

Full-size pattern

Unicorn

The Unicorn was made from preprimed MDF, but solid wood can also be used.

Supplies
¾"-thick MDF: 12" x 16"
⅛"- to ¼"-thick plywood: 12" x 16"
Basic Tools & Supplies from page 15

Instructions
See Segmentation Technique Instructions on pages 16–28.

I. Prepare the Patterns.
1. Apply one Unicorn pattern from page 69 to pine.

II. Cut the Wood.
1. See Photo No. 8-9.

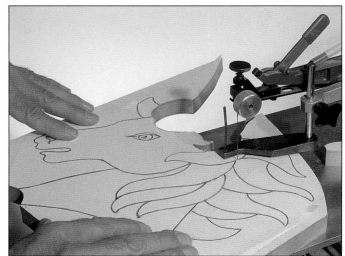

Photo No. 8-9   Cut the Unicorn into segments.

III. Shape & Smooth the Wood.

1. Reduce the inner ear thickness ¼" and do not round its edges.

2. Round-over all other segments about ¼" or ⁵⁄₁₆" radius, except the inner eye which is about ⅛" radius. See Photos No. 8-10 and No. 8-11.

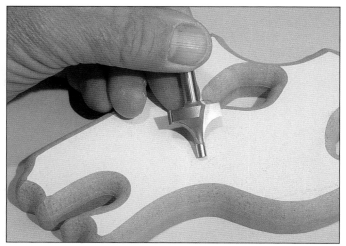

Photo No. 8-10   This carbide-tipped router bit with its very small pilot (just ⁵⁄₃₂" diameter) is ideal for getting into tight corners.

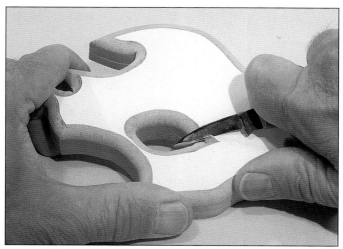

Photo No. 8-11   Use a knife to round the edges of the inside corner of the Unicorn's eye.

IV. Color & Finish the Segments.

1. Paint the inner ear gray before assembly.

V. Assemble the Segments.

1. Sand and glue all segments edge to edge before painting. See Photo No. 8-12.

Photo No. 8-12   All shaping to the individual segments is completed. The project is now ready for assembly and painting.

VI. Make a Backer.

1. Paint the entire project.

2. Paint the inside of the nostril and the eye black. Paint the horn gold and apply some gold or silver glitter.

Design Tip

If making the Unicorn from solid wood, make it from two pieces: one ¾" x 1½" x 7" for the horn and another piece ¾" x 12" x 12" for the head. Notice the recommended grain orientation given on the Unicorn pattern on opposite page for the solid wood construction.

UNICORN
Design by Patricia Spielman

Enlarge 200% for full-size pattern

NOTE: If using solid wood, make from two pieces, each with the grain as indicated by the arrows.

HORN Grain

-1/4"

HEAD Grain

Chapter 9
Nautical
Projects

Nautical designs are always very popular and the four projects presented here are certainly classic subjects—mermaid, lighthouse, anchor, and sailboat. In addition, instructions for two different methods of roping the edges of the project plaques are included on pages 80–83.

The technique for making wood look like patina-aged metal, using an easy-to-apply finish, is also provided with the instructions for making the segmented anchor project.

Mermaid

Supplies
¾"-thick clear pine: 7" x 9⅜" for oval plaque
⅛"- to ¼"-thick Baltic birch plywood: 4" x 8"
Basic Tools & Supplies from page 15
Sawtooth hanger

Instructions
See Segmentation Technique Instructions on pages 16–28.

I. Prepare the Patterns.
1. Apply one Mermaid pattern from opposite page to Baltic birch plywood.

II. Cut the Wood.
1. Cut a 7" x 9⅜" oval plaque from clear pine.

III. Shape & Smooth the Wood.
1. Round-over all edges about ¹⁄₁₆" radius.

IV. Color & Finish the Segments.

V. Assemble the Segments.
1. Glue the segments, one at a time, directly onto the plaque.

2. Rope the plaque edge according to Making Rope-edged Plaques instructions on pages 80–83. An alternative is to rout a decorative edge around the plaque.

3. Add a sawtooth hanger to the back.

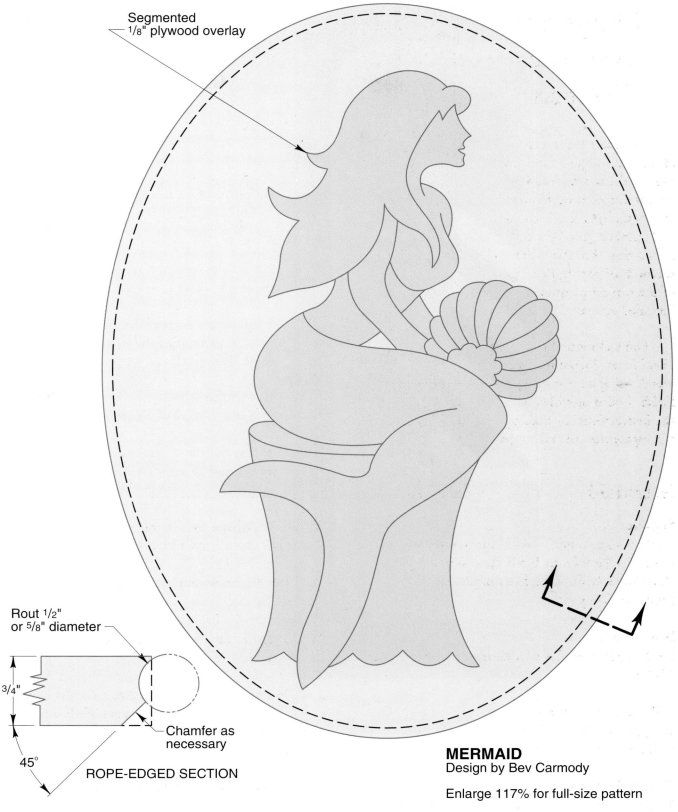

Segmented
1/8" plywood overlay

Rout 1/2"
or 5/8" diameter

3/4"

45°

Chamfer as
necessary

ROPE-EDGED SECTION

MERMAID
Design by Bev Carmody

Enlarge 117% for full-size pattern

71

Lighthouse

This project is a segmented version of North Carolina's Cape Hatteras Lighthouse, the tallest and probably the most famous lighthouse in America.

Supplies

¾"-thick ash: 7" x 14½" for plaque
¾"-thick clear pine: 4¼" x 13¼"
Basic Tools & Supplies from page 15
Sawtooth hanger

Instructions

See Segmentation Technique Instructions on pages 16–28.

I. Prepare the Patterns.

1. Apply one Lighthouse pattern from pages 73–74 to clear pine.

2. Cut one pattern horizontally, removing the center main tower section.

3. Apply the patterns for the top and bottom sections to the work piece in their respective positions.

II. Cut the Wood.

1. Cut a 7" x 14½" plaque from ash.

2. Cut out the central tower section so it is one complete unit (not individual segments).

III. Shape & Smooth the Wood.

1. Use a hand plane or a power abrasive tool to taper the central main tower from a thickness of ¾" at the bottom to ½" at the top.

2. Round-over the edges of the main tower before applying the pattern to it with a temporary bonding spray adhesive.

3. Complete the cutting process, cutting the sections into individual segments.

4. Reduce the segments to the appropriate thickness as specified on the pattern.

5. Round-over and/or chamfer the edges as appropriate.

IV. Color & Finish the Segments.

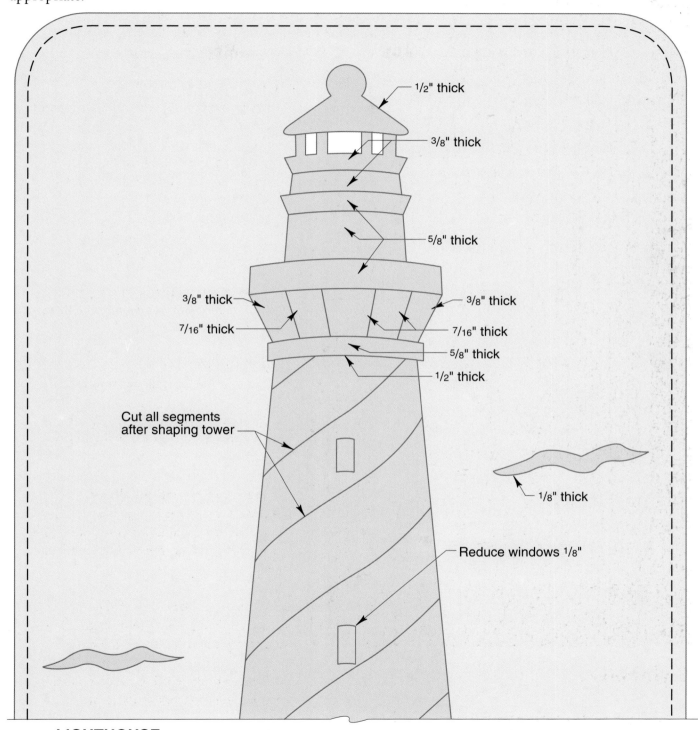

1/2" thick

3/8" thick

5/8" thick

3/8" thick

3/8" thick

7/16" thick

7/16" thick

5/8" thick

1/2" thick

Cut all segments after shaping tower

1/8" thick

Reduce windows 1/8"

LIGHTHOUSE
Design by Patricia Spielman

Full-size pattern

73

V. Assemble the Segments.

1. Glue the segments, one at a time, directly onto the plaque.

2. Rope the plaque edge according to Making Rope-edged Plaques instructions on pages 80–83. An alternative is to rout a decorative edge around the plaque.

3. Add a sawtooth hanger onto the back.

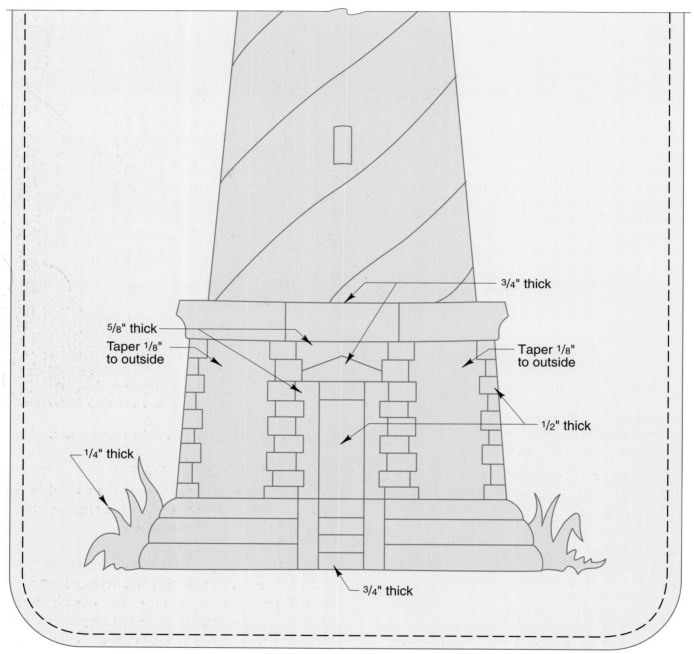

3/4" thick

5/8" thick
Taper 1/8" to outside

Taper 1/8" to outside

1/2" thick

1/4" thick

3/4" thick

LIGHTHOUSE
Design by Patricia Spielman

Full-size pattern

Plaque
3/4" x 7" x 14 1/2"

Antique Anchor

This stunning project appears far more difficult to make than it actually is.

Supplies
¾"-thick clear pine: 7" x 9⅜" for oval plaque
¾"-thick straight-grained soft wood: 5¾" x 7¾"
Basic Tools & Supplies from page 15
Sawtooth hanger

Instructions
See Segmentation Technique Instructions on pages 16–28.

I. Prepare the Patterns.
1. Apply one Antique Anchor pattern from page 77 to clear pine.

II. Cut the Wood.

1. Cut a 7" x 9⅜" oval plaque from clear pine.

III. Shape & Smooth the Wood.
1. Reduce the thickness of segments indicated on the pattern. **Note:** Concentrating on one segment at a time makes round-over work easier.

2. Chamfer the edges of the diamond-shaped segment to match those of the adjoining segments at the bottom. **Note:** The segments are correctly shaped so that when assembled, the anchor appears to have a continuous v-groove carved in the center of it. See Photo No. 9-1 on page 76.

75

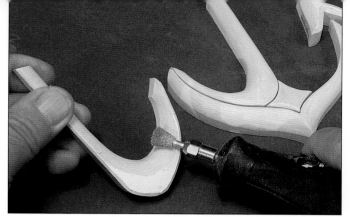

Photo No. 9-1   Shape a segment of the anchor using a rotary tool with a structured carbide cutter.

3. Shape the rope segments with carved v-grooves. Round-over the corners by hand. See Photos No. 9-2 and No. 9-3.

Photo No. 9-2   Shape the carved rope beginning with a series of slanted knife cuts to make v-grooves.

IV. Color & Finish the Segments.

1. Glue anchor segments together one at a time. See Photo No. 9-3.

Photo No. 9-3   The anchor carving is complete. Glue the anchor segments together prior to finishing.

76

2. For a weathered look, use a three-step, water-based green patina finish. See Photos No. 9-4 and No. 9-5.

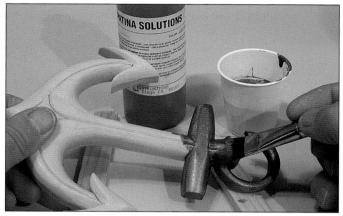

Photo No. 9-4   The first step to a metallic patina finish is to apply liquid copper (or brass) finish over a sealer.

Photo No. 9-5   The patina solution, applied with a sponge, changes the look of the copper.

V. Assemble the Segments.

1. Glue the assembled anchor segments directly onto the plaque.

2. Rope the plaque edge according to Making Rope-edged Plaques instructions on page 80–83. An alternative is to rout a decorative edge around the plaque.

3. Add a sawtooth hanger to the back.

Design Tip

As an option, you can choose to omit the segments of hand-carved rope. In this case, change the pattern so it has a complete ring at the top.

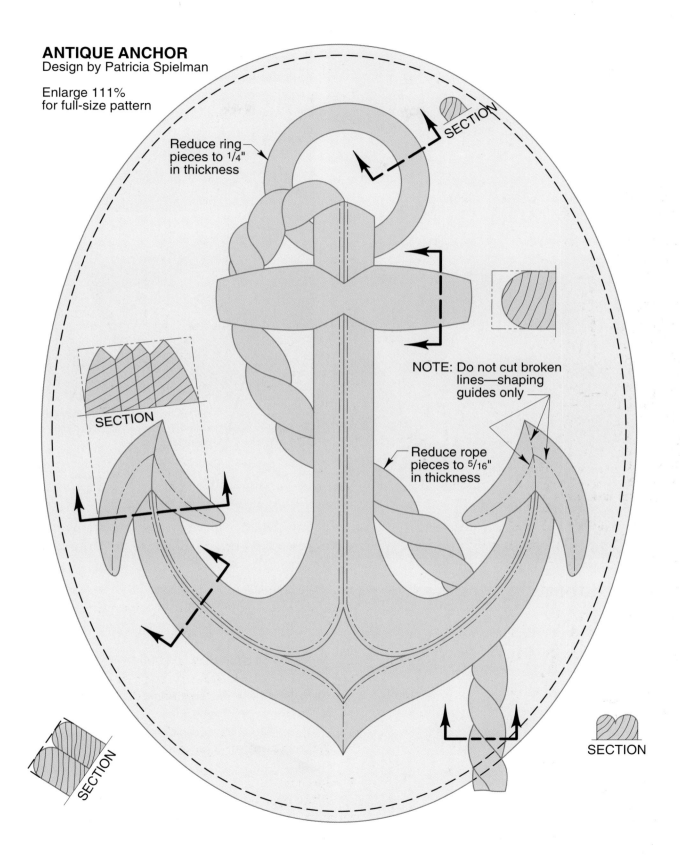

ANTIQUE ANCHOR
Design by Patricia Spielman

Enlarge 111%
for full-size pattern

Reduce ring
pieces to 1/4"
in thickness

SECTION

NOTE: Do not cut broken
lines—shaping
guides only

Reduce rope
pieces to 5/16"
in thickness

SECTION

SECTION

SECTION

Sculpted Sailboat

This project is more carving than segmentation since only one of the sails is cut into four segments.

Supplies
¾"-thick ash: 7" x 9⅜" for oval plaque
⅞"-thick pine: 5" x 6¼"; 1" x 5"
Basic Tools & Supplies from page 15
Sawtooth hanger

Instructions
See Segmentation Technique Instructions on pages 16–28.

I. Prepare the Patterns.
1. Apply one Sculpted Sailboat pattern from opposite page to pine.

II. Cut the Wood.
1. Rough-shape all segments first by compound-sawing them. See Photo No. 9-6.

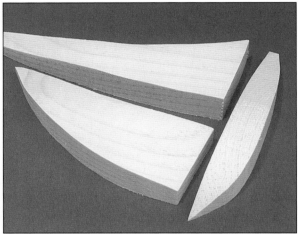

Photo No. 9-6   Rough-cut segments to shape by compound-sawing with the scroll saw and/or with the help of a disc or belt sander.

2. Cut a 7" x 9⅜" oval from ash.

III. Shape & Smooth the Wood.
1. Carefully remove the profile pattern after compound-sawing. Round-over the front sail.

2. Reapply the pattern.

3. Cut out the segments.

IV. Color & Finish the Segments.

V. Assemble the Segments.
1. Rope the plaque edge according to Making Rope-edged Plaques instructions on pages 80–83. An alternative is to rout a decorative edge around the plaque.

2. Add a sawtooth hanger onto the back.

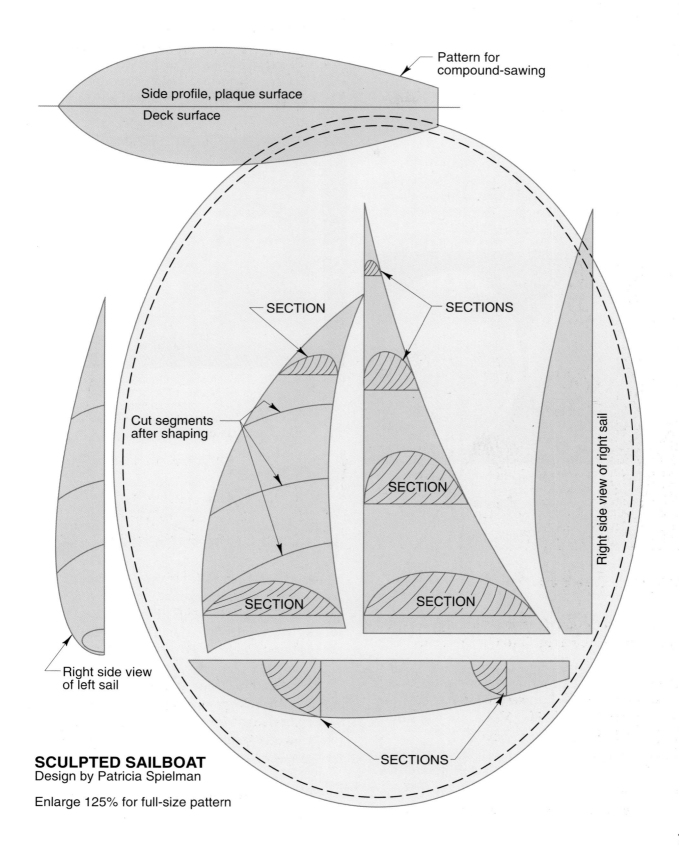

Pattern for compound-sawing

Side profile, plaque surface

Deck surface

SECTION

SECTIONS

Cut segments after shaping

SECTION

SECTION

SECTION

Right side view of right sail

Right side view of left sail

SECTIONS

SCULPTED SAILBOAT
Design by Patricia Spielman

Enlarge 125% for full-size pattern

Making Rope-edged Plaques

In addition to the nautical plaques, you can use the rope-edged technique to embellish western plaques and various signs. Most rope-edged plaques look shoddy because the ends are usually crudely butted. Here are two different techniques for perfecting rope edging on plaques, using two kinds of rope. One method magically conceals the rope ends, making the rope look endless. This technique is more involved than the other, but it is certainly worth the extra effort. See Photo No. 9-7.

Photo No. 9-7   Shown are two methods of perfecting the roped edge, using two types of rope: sisal-hemp rope on the left with a retwisting technique appears endless. The nylon rope on the right has a simple glued butt joint that is barely visible. The pencils point to rope ends.

Ropes

Most hardware stores sell three types of rope: 1) sisal hemp rope; 2) white nylon rope; and 3) yellow polypropylene rope. Ropes are also either twisted or braided. Avoid polypropylene and braided ropes.

1. Select a rope size (diameter) that complements the thickness of the wooden plaque. For example, use ⅝" rope with ¾" plaques. If mounted flush to the front surface of the plaque, ¾" or ½" rope also will work.

Preparing the Plaques

1. Cut boards to round or oval shapes. Round the corners on square, triangular, or other geometric shapes so the rope does not have to make a sharp bend.

2. Using a ⅜"-diameter round-nose bit and a router table, rout a ⅛"-deep groove into the edge of the plaque to cradle the rope. See the detail of the Rope-edged Section on the Mermaid pattern on page 71. See Photo No. 9-8. This groove will accommodate ½"- to ¾"-diameter rope.

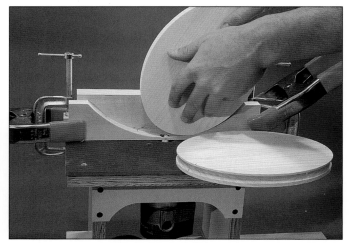

Photo No. 9-8   Rout a shallow round-bottomed groove around the edge of the plaque to "seat" the rope, using a router table.

3. Clamp a concave-edged board to the fence to support the work piece over the bit, assuring a uniform depth of cut.

4. Slightly offset the groove toward the front of the plaque. Rout with the front surface facing away from the fence and keep the stock moving into the bit.

5. Clamp a piece of thin plywood to a table that has a zero-clearance hole surrounding the bit. This will help when routing the edge grooves around rounded corners and connecting straight edges of square and rectangular plaques.

Alternatively, shallow v-grooves can be fabricated around plaque edges by gluing two pieces of wood, back to back, that have previously cut bevel-cut edges. Upon completion of the process, an inverted v-edge will have been formed all around.

Chamfering & Finishing

1. Chamfer the edge on the back of the plaque next

to the groove when premade loops of rope will be stretch-fit into the grooves. See the detail of the Rope-edged Section on the Mermaid pattern on page 71. Plaques roped with butted ends do not require chamfering.

2. Completely finish plaques before applying the rope edging. Leave surfaces of the groove unfinished where you may want to glue the rope into the groove.

Preparing the Rope

For convenience sake, the two different techniques for mounting rope to plaque edges have been named as "glue-butting" and "retwisting." Each technique requires different preparation. Both nylon and sisal ropes can be used for the glue-butting technique, but only sisal rope works well for the retwisting process. A thin-consistency instant glue is necessary for the glue-butting method and helpful for the retwisting technique.

Glue-butting

Just as the name implies, the rope is glued end-to-end with instant glue. This method leaves a visible glue line, but is the quickest and easiest technique for both sisal and nylon ropes. The key is to keep the ends from fraying.

1. Using a clear, low-viscosity, instant adhesive, saturate the cutting areas. See Photo No. 9-9.

Photo No. 9-9   The secret to eliminating fraying and un-raveling is to plasticize the rope with an instant glue before cutting it. Notice how the nylon strands lose their shape compared to those of the sisal rope when untwisted.

Note: The adhesive sets in a few seconds, allowing the rope to be cut on the scroll saw without fraying. See Photo No. 9-10. Using the adhesive to plasticize the rope allows you to work it almost like wood or plastic.

Photo No. 9-10   Cut the rope on the scroll saw. A thin board taped to the table supports the rope over the table opening around the blade.

2. Square one end of the rope. Measure, mark, cut, square to length, and assemble. See Photos No. 9-11 through 9-14 below and on page 82.

Photo No. 9-11   Mark the rope where ends butt.

Photo No. 9-12   This piece of nylon rope has sharp, clean, and square cuts, making it ready for gluing end to end.

Photo No. 9-13   The rope now has a glued-butt joint. Use a craft knife to cut away any glue "squeeze out" and to shape the joint.

Photo No. 9-14   Shown here is a completed butt joint on sisal rope.

3. Apply a gap-filling instant glue or epoxy into the plaque groove. Place one end of the rope into the glue-filled groove. Tightly pull the other end to it, matching the twists of the rope, and glue the joint. **Note:** A gap-filling instant glue is ideal for this job because it sets quick. It is best to locate the butt joint at the bottom of the plaque where light shadows will help to hide the joint.

Retwisting

This technique requires three times the amount of rope to edge one plaque, but it creates a wonderful-looking edge that appears to be endless. Although this method is not difficult, it is recommended to make some practice loops first.

Use sisal rope and select one with strands that hold their shape well when separated. Nylon strands become very limp and flimsy when separated, making a neat retwisting job impossible.

1. Measure the optimum length of rope required. See Photo No. 9-11 on page 81. Mark all three strands clearly.

2. Cut the rope to three times the measured length. See Photos No. 9-10 on page 81 and No. 9-15.

Photo No. 9-15   A length that is three times the circumference is required.

Note: It helps to give the rope a light dose of thin instant glue at the cut ends so the strand ends still separate from each other but do not fray or unravel.

3. Now separate the rope into three individual strands. See Photo No. 9-16.

Photo No. 9-16   Separate the rope into three individual strands.

4. Starting at the previously marked one-third point of the total length, retwist one strand to form a two-strand loop. It is helpful to place a drop of glue at this point, under the starting end.

5. Tightly and uniformly pull the two strands together as you continue to retwist the strands, forming a two-strand loop. See Photo No. 9-17.

Photo No. 9-17   Retwist one strand to make what appears to be an endless loop of three-strand rope.

6. Continue retwisting until you have created a loop of three-strand rope. See Photo No. 9-18.

Photo No. 9-18   The completed loop of twisted rope has only the ends of one of the three new strands butting together, which can be concealed against the wood in the groove.

7. Prepare the plaque with a shallow groove. Be certain to chamfer the back edge to facilitate stretching the rope onto the edge of the plaque.

8. Stretch the loop onto the plaque. If the loop is too large you can undo it and start again. If the loop is too small you can reduce the size of the plaque until it fits. See Photo No. 9-19.

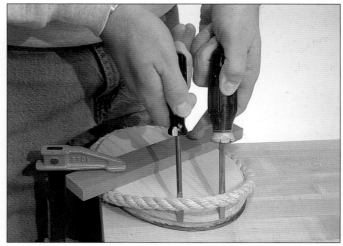

Photo No. 9-19   Using two screwdrivers for leverage, force a rope loop onto a plaque with the plaque face down.

Chapter 10
Nostalgic Projects

"First Kiss," "Big Catch," and "Woman with Basket" are all standing designs by R. Stephan Toman that have similar construction details.

First Kiss

Supplies
⅞"- to 1⅛"-thick pine: 6" x 16"
¾"-thick pine: 2" x 9½"
Basic Tools & Supplies from page 15

Instructions
See Segmentation Technique Instructions on pages 16–28.

I. Prepare the Patterns.
1. Apply one First Kiss pattern from opposite page to large piece of pine.

II. Cut the Wood.

III. Shape & Smooth the Wood.
1. Round-over all edges.

2. Use a wood-burning tool to texture the boy's hair. See Photo No. 10-1.

Photo No. 10-1   The boy's hair segment is tapered toward the top and then textured with a wood-burning tool.

IV. Color & Finish the Segments.

V. Assemble the Segments. & VI. Make a Backer.
1. Cut mortises into the base as indicated.

2. Insert the scroll-sawn tenons into mortises cut into the base. See Photo No. 10-2.

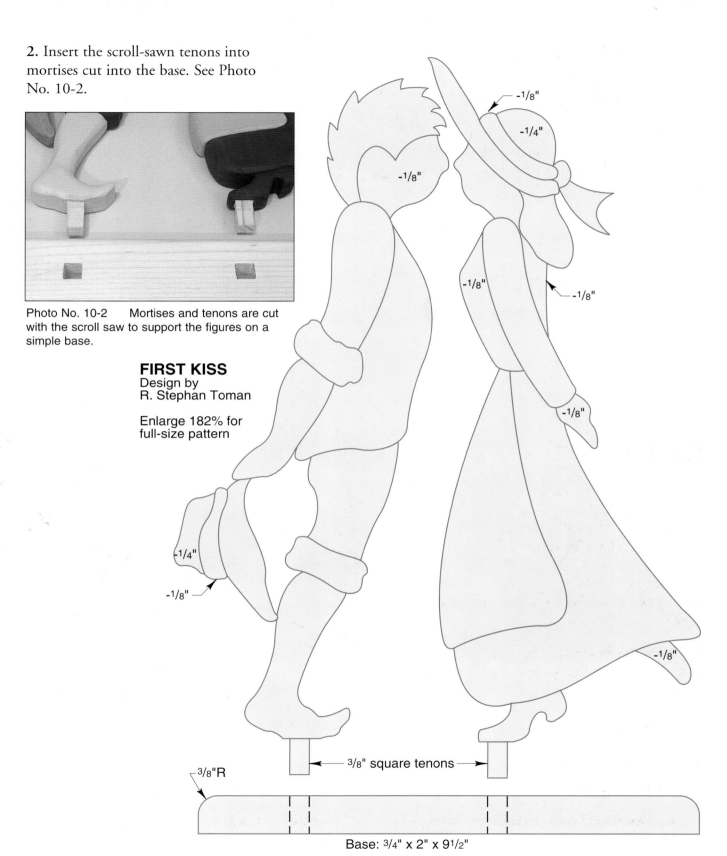

Photo No. 10-2   Mortises and tenons are cut with the scroll saw to support the figures on a simple base.

FIRST KISS
Design by
R. Stephan Toman

Enlarge 182% for
full-size pattern

-1/8"

-1/8"

-1/4"

-1/8"

-1/8"

-1/8"

-1/4"

-1/8"

-1/8"

-1/8"

3/8" square tenons

3/8"R

Base: 3/4" x 2" x 9 1/2"

Big Catch

Supplies
⅞"- to 1⅛"-thick pine: 5" x 9"
¾"-thick pine: 2¼" x 6¼"
⅛"-diameter dowel: 6¾" long
Basic Tools & Supplies from page 15

Instructions
See Segmentation Technique Instructions on pages 16–28.

I. Prepare the Patterns.
1. Apply one Big Catch pattern from page 88 to large piece of pine.

II. Cut the Wood.

III. Shape & Smooth the Wood.
1. Round-over all edges. See Photo No. 10-3 on opposite page.

Photo No. 10-3   Here, segments have been cut out and round-over work has begun, using a high-speed rotary tool.

2. Taper the dowel fishing pole. See Photo No. 10-4.

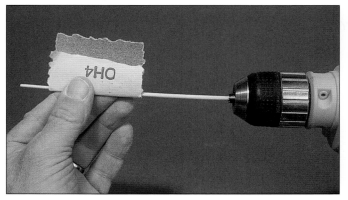

Photo No. 10-4   Taper the ⅛"-diameter dowel with abrasive paper.

IV. Color & Finish the Segments.

V. Assemble the Segments. & VI. Make a Backer.

1. Cut mortises into the base as indicated.

2. Insert the scroll-sawn tenons into mortises cut into the base. See Photo No. 10-2 on page 85.

3. Glue the dowel between the two backer pieces for a double-sided project. See Photo No. 10-5. For a front-facing project, glue it to the back side just above the boy's shoulder.

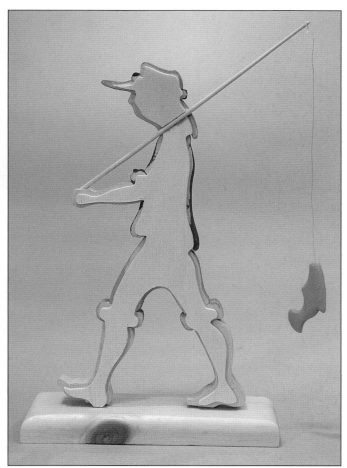

Photo No. 10-5   The two-piece backer is cut from ⅛" plywood and glued in place on each side of the dowel fishing pole.

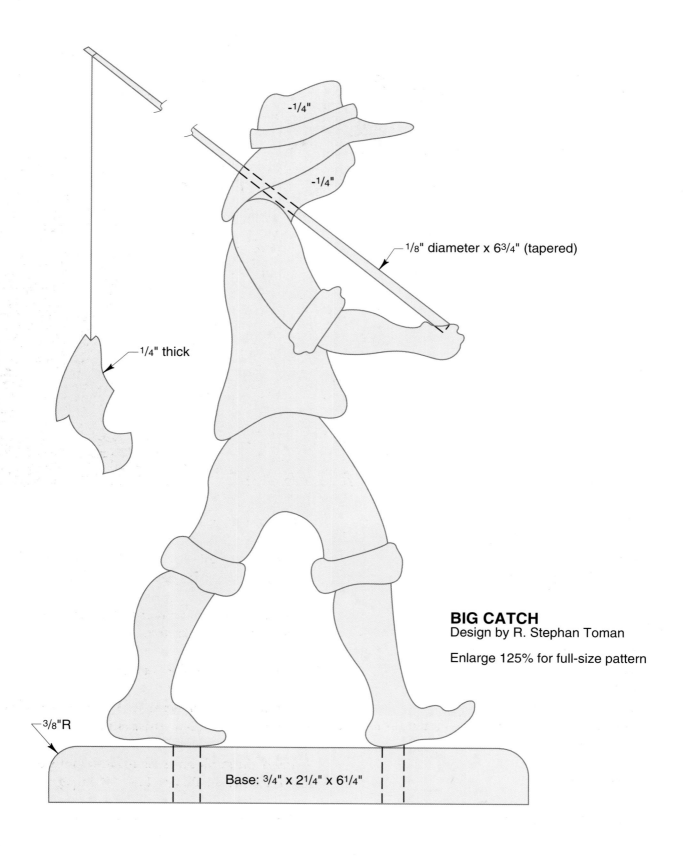

-1/4"

-1/4"

1/8" diameter x 6³/4" (tapered)

1/4" thick

BIG CATCH
Design by R. Stephan Toman

Enlarge 125% for full-size pattern

3/8"R

Base: ³/4" x 2¹/4" x 6¹/4"

Woman
with Basket

Supplies
⅞"- to 1⅛"-thick pine: 8" x 9"
¾"-thick pine: 3½" x 10"
Basic Tools & Supplies from page 15
Drywall screw: 1¼"

Instructions
See Segmentation Technique Instructions on pages
16–28.

I. Prepare the Patterns.
1. Apply one Woman with Basket pattern from page
90 to large piece of pine.

II. Cut the Wood.

III. Shape & Smooth the Wood.

1. Round-over all edges.

2. Reduce the basket's handle thickness in the front
and back to make it appear more realistic.

3. Use a wood-burning tool to form the basket-
weave lines into the surface of the basket.

IV. Color & Finish the Segments.

V. Assemble the Segments. & VI. Make a Backer.
1. Cut mortises into the base as indicated.

2. Insert the scroll-sawn tenons into mortises cut
into the base. See Photo No. 10-2 on page 85.

3. Attach the basket with the drywall screw.

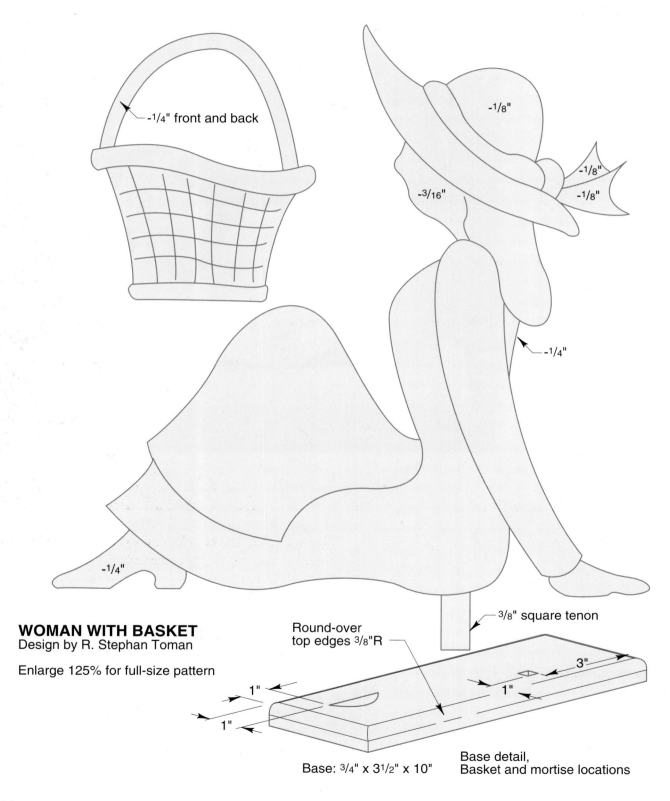

-1/4" front and back

-1/8"

-3/16"

-1/8"

-1/8"

-1/4"

-1/4"

WOMAN WITH BASKET
Design by R. Stephan Toman

Enlarge 125% for full-size pattern

Round-over
top edges 3/8"R

3/8" square tenon

1"

1"

3"

1"

Base: 3/4" x 3 1/2" x 10"

Base detail,
Basket and mortise locations

Chapter 11
Country
Projects

These segmented projects, with a feel for the country, demonstrate the effects of applying a variety of finishing options. Selected woods can be finished all-natural, enhanced with a stain or dye, colored with acrylic paints, or completed with a combination of any of these.

Small Rooster

This is a double-sided free-standing project that is made from one piece of wood with a combination of painted and natural finishes.

Supplies
¾"- to ⅞"-thick poplar: 5½" x 7"
¾"-thick pine: 3" x 4" for base
¼"-diameter dowel: 2" (2)
Basic Tools & Supplies from page 15

Instructions
See Segmentation Technique Instructions on pages 16–28.

I. Prepare the Patterns.
1. Apply one Small Rooster pattern from page 92 to poplar.

2. Layout the dowel holes and drill them. See Photos No. 5-4 and No. 5-5 on page 38.

II. Cut the Wood.

III. Shape & Smooth the Wood.
1. Chamfer and sand all edges on both sides of Small Rooster segments.

IV. Color & Finish the Segments.

V. Assemble the Segments.

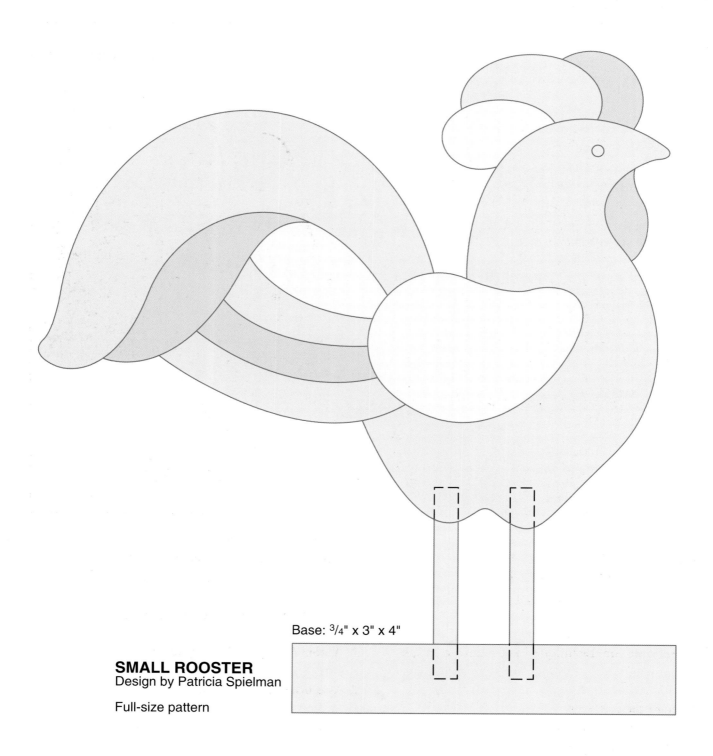

Base: ³/₄" x 3" x 4"

SMALL ROOSTER
Design by Patricia Spielman

Full-size pattern

Rooster Plaques

Supplies
¾"-thick pine: 11" x 15"; 10½" x 15"
⅛"- to ¼"-thick plywood: 11" x 15"; 10½" x 15"
Basic Tools & Supplies from page 15

Instructions
See Segmentation Technique Instructions on pages 16–28.

I. Prepare the Patterns.
1. Apply one of each Rooster Plaques pattern from pages 94 and 95 to pine.

II. Cut the Wood.

III. Shape & Smooth the Wood.
1. If desired, reduce the thickness of the feet, the combs, and the wattles (under the beak) ³⁄₁₆".

2. Round-over all edges about ³⁄₁₆" radius.

IV. Color & Finish the Segments.

V. Assemble the Segments.

VI. Make a Backer.

ROOSTER PLAQUES
Design by Patricia Spielman

Enlarge 200% for full-size pattern

ROOSTER PLAQUES
Design by Patricia Spielman

Enlarge 200% for full-size pattern

Segmented Sunflower

This is an easy and fun-to-make project that is made from inexpensive pine.

Supplies
¾"-thick pine: 9" x 26¼"
⅛"-thick plywood: 9" x 26¼"
Basic Tools & Supplies from page 15

Instructions
See Segmentation Technique Instructions on pages 16–28.

I. Prepare the Patterns.

1. Apply one Segmented Sunflower pattern from pages 97–98 to pine.

II. Cut the Wood.
1. Leave the pattern paper on the wood until sanding, as this will indicate the face or upper side of the segments.

2. Notice that the pattern has two lines around the center of the flower. Cut on the outer line around the center of the flower. Sand to the inside line, reducing the size of the center segment. **Note:** This will allow the surrounding petals to slide in further toward the center and thus reduce open gaps resulting from the many saw kerfs made when cutting out all of the petal segments.

III. Shape & Smooth the Wood.
1. Use your imagination and intuition when shaping the petals. Most should taper in thickness inward toward the center of the flower. Give all petals, with the exception of the four "A" petals, a sideways slant. See the petal shaping sketches on the Segmented Sunflower pattern on opposite page.

2. Reduce the four "B" petals to ½" thickness.

3. Round-over all edges of the petals to ⅛" radius.

4. Round-over the edges of the center of the segment to ⅜" radius.

5. Taper the stem from ¾" thickness at the bottom to ½" where it meets the petals.

6. Leave one edge on each of the leaf segments sharp and round-over the other edge to ⅜" radius. See the Segmented Sunflower pattern on page 98.

7. Reduce the remaining segments of each leaf to ½" thickness and round-over all edges to ¼" radius.

IV. Color & Finish the Segments.

V. Assemble the Segments.

VI. Make a Backer.

SEGMENTED SUNFLOWER
Design by Patricia Spielman

Enlarge 117% for full-size pattern

NOTE: Reduce "B" petals to 1/2" in thickness

B

B

A

A

B

A

Cut on outside line, sand to inside line

A

A

B

"A" petals

Double slant

Typical petal shapes before rounding over

A — A

1/8" plywood backing

Typical section through center of flower

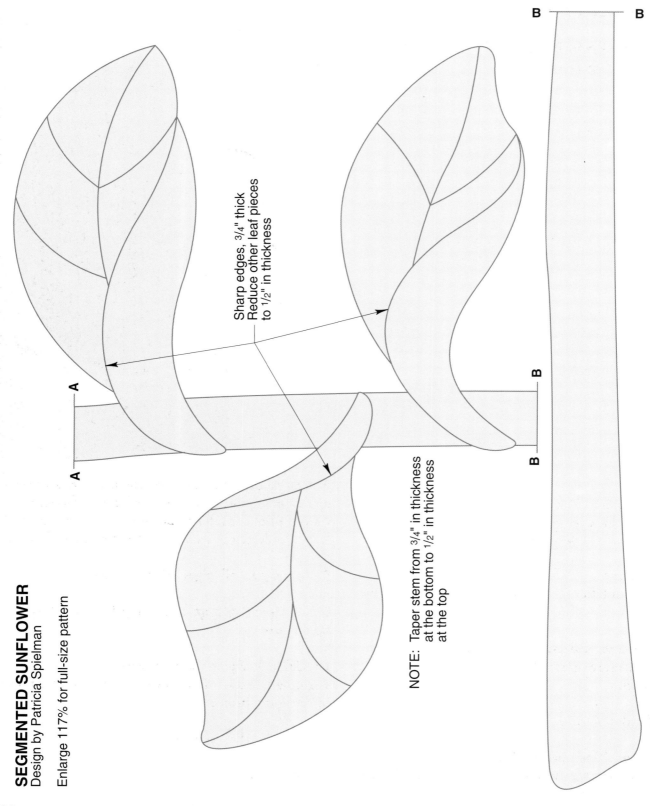

SEGMENTED SUNFLOWER
Design by Patricia Spielman

Enlarge 117% for full-size pattern

Sharp edges, 3/4" thick
Reduce other leaf pieces
to 1/2" in thickness

A

A

B

B

B

B

B

B

NOTE: Taper stem from 3/4" in thickness
at the bottom to 1/2" in thickness
at the top

Segmented Pony

This design by Bev Carmody was cut from a single piece of pine.

Supplies
¾"-thick pine: 10" x 17"
⅛"- to ¼"-thick plywood: 10" x 17"
Basic Tools & Supplies from page 15

Instructions
See Segmentation Technique Instructions on pages 16–28.

I. Prepare the Patterns.
1. Apply one Segmented Pony pattern from page 100 to pine.

II. Cut the Wood.

III. Shape & Smooth the Wood.
1. Reduce the thickness of segments indicated with a minus (-) sign on the pattern.

2. Using a belt or disc sander, shape the grassy leaves by beveling and/or tapering the front surfaces in various directions, following arrows on the pattern which indicate the recommended direction of slope.

3. Round-over all edges ¹⁄₁₆" to ⅛" radius.

4. Finish-sand all segments, using 150- or 180-grit sand paper.

IV. Color & Finish the Segments.
1. Apply a coat of clear polyurethane or acrylic finish to the entire project.

V. Assemble the Segments.

VI. Make a Backer.

SEGMENTED PONY
Design by Bev Carmody

Enlarge 182% for full-size pattern

NOTE: - Indicates material thickness reduction
       → Indicates bevel/tapering direction

100

Chapter 12
Home Decor

The segmented embellishment of these projects gives new dimension to interior decorations.

The mirror is crafted from a single piece of nicely figured, natural-finished wood. The "quilted" wood project, on the other hand, makes a bold statement in any room with its randomly raised segments and sponge-applied finish that creates a mottled pattern and the look of fabric.

Heart in Home

Supplies
¼"-thick Baltic Birch plywood: 7⅞" x 10⅛"
¼"-thick plywood: 7⅞" x 9⅞"
Basic Tools & Supplies from page 15
Sponges: ¾" x 3¼" x 5½" (2)

Instructions
See Segmentation Technique Instructions on pages 16–28.

I. Prepare the Patterns.
1. Apply one Heart in Home pattern from opposite page to Baltic Birch plywood.

II. Cut the Wood.

III. Shape & Smooth the Wood.
1. Chamfer all edges ⅟₁₆".

IV. Color & Finish the Segments.
1. Prime all segments on the front surfaces and on the chamfered edges. Do not prime the back surfaces—leave those unfinished for gluing.

2. Paint each of the segments with acrylic paints in the primary color; ie., if the segment is predominantly red (like the six heart segments), paint it red. Allow paint to dry.

3. Cut a sponge into small squares. See Photo No. 12-1.

Photo No. 12-1   Cut a sponge into small workable pieces.

102

4. Wet the sponge and squeeze out excess water. Prepare the complementary acrylic paint color to the consistency of ketchup.

5. Press the moistened sponge into the paint, and blot the sponge onto paper towels to test the texturing effect and remove excess paint from the sponge.

6. Lightly press the sponge to the work surface in a vertical direction with a straight up-and-down daubing motion. **Note:** Moving sideways will create a smeared look. If you do not like the look of your sponge work, just wipe away the new coat of paint before it dries and repaint. See Photo No. 12-2.

Photo No. 12-2   Using a sponge to apply acrylic paint creates an unusual texture.

7. Add a second color by repeating Steps 3–6 with a different complementary color. **Note:** This was done to the segment surrounding the large red heart and the two hearts in the corner, where red and yellow were sponged over a base of light green.

V. Assemble the Segments. & VI. Make a Backer.
1. Glue the outside frame segment to a backer. Allow it to set before gluing down the remaining segments.

2. Apply a coat of nongloss water-based polyurethane.

HEART IN HOME

Design by Frank Droege

Enlarge 165% for full-size pattern

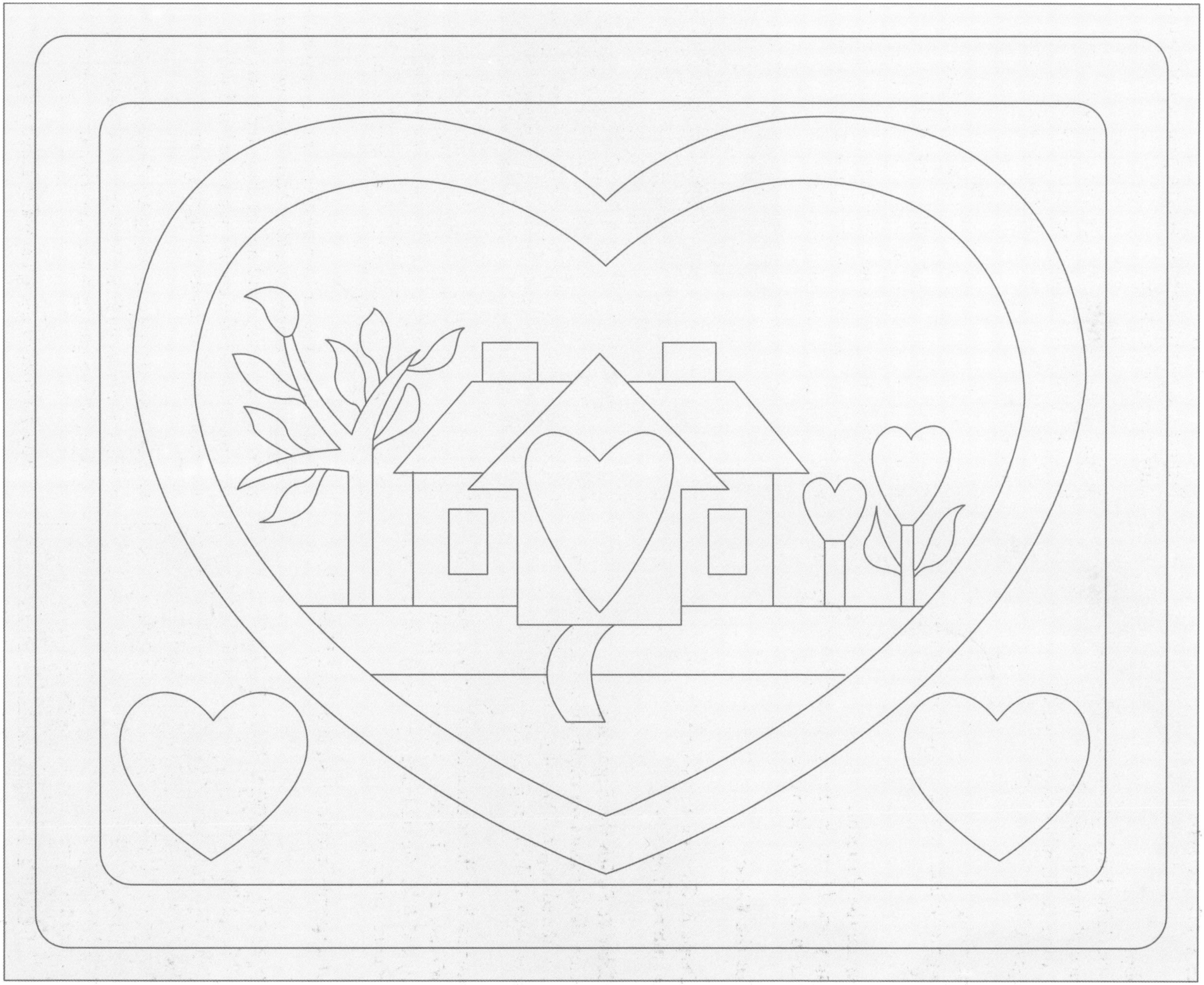

III. Shape & Smooth the Wood.

1. Round-over the edges, following the small arrows on the petals of the flower in the pattern, suggesting an optional tapering toward the center.

IV. Color & Finish the Segments.

1. Apply a coat of nongloss water-based polyurethane.

V. Assemble the Segments.

VI. Make a Backer.

1. Use the backer to mark the shape on the mirror. See Photo No. 12-3.

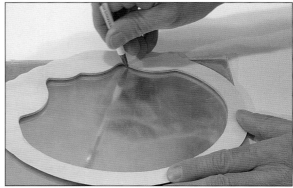

Photo No. 12-3   Using the plywood backer as a pattern, lay out the cutting line for the acrylic mirror.

Segmented Mirror

Supplies
¾"-thick butternut: 8½" x 10¼"
⅛" to ¼"-thick acrylic mirror: 6½" x 8"
Basic Tools & Supplies from page 15

Instructions
See Segmentation Technique Instructions on pages 16–28.

I. Prepare the Patterns.
1. Apply one Segmented Mirror pattern from opposite page to butternut.

II. Cut the Wood.

Note: A ballpoint pen will mark the front of the mirror. There is no protective covering on the back side, so it is very important to avoid scratching it.

2. Cut out the mirror. **Note:** It is best to use a piece of lightweight cardboard under the acrylic to protect it during cutting. Hold cardboard in place with masking tape pulled over onto the front of the mirror. Do not allow the tape to come in contact with the mirror backing as it may pull off the reflective coating when removed.

3. Insert the mirror and secure it to the wood with a small bead of adhesive.

104

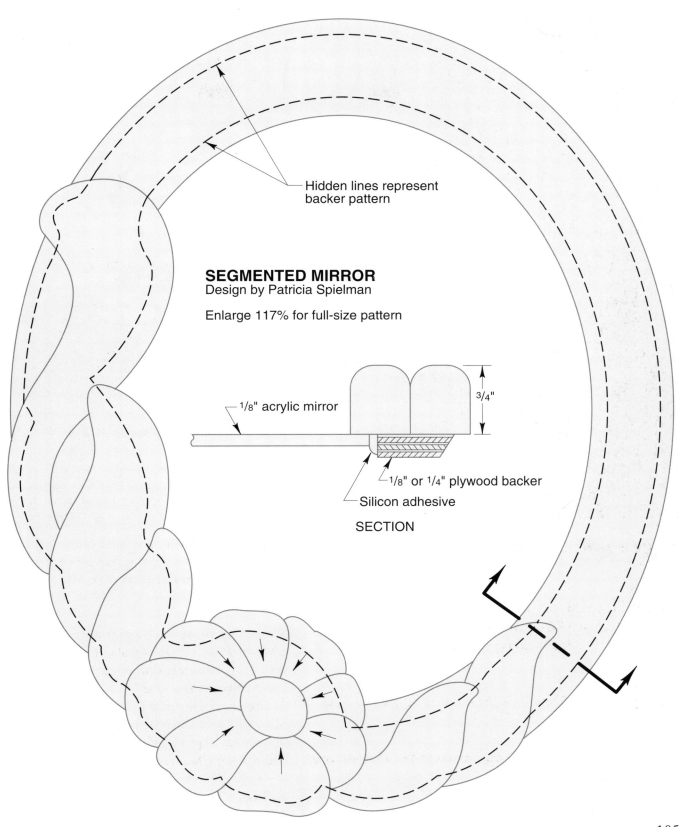

Hidden lines represent
backer pattern

SEGMENTED MIRROR
Design by Patricia Spielman

Enlarge 117% for full-size pattern

3/4"

1/8" acrylic mirror

1/8" or 1/4" plywood backer

Silicon adhesive

SECTION

Chapter 13
Separated
Segmentation

Separated segmentation differs from regular segmentation in that the thin plywood backer is intentionally made to be a visible part of the project. The backer is painted black or any other contrasting color and exposed all around the edges and between the brightly painted segments.

Luv Bugs

This colorful and charming design by Aaron Moriarity is perfect for a child's room. Remember, the pattern can be enlarged to suit.

Supplies
¼"-thick Baltic birch plywood: 10" x 14½"
⅛"- to ¼"-thick Baltic birch plywood: 10" x 14½"
Basic Tools & Supplies from page 15

Instructions
See Segmentation Technique Instructions on pages 16–28.

I. Prepare the Patterns.
1. Apply one Luv Bugs pattern from pages 107–108 to each piece of Baltic birch plywood.

II. Cut the Wood.
1. Cut out the backer to shape.

2. Cut out all of the segments.

III. Shape & Smooth the Wood.
1. Slightly round-over all edges to ⅟₁₆" radius.

IV. Color & Finish the Segments. & VI. Make a Backer.
1. Using a craft knife, cut away the pattern where the backer will be painted. See Photo No. 13-1.

Photo No. 13-1   The areas of the backer to be painted are cut away from the pattern while it is still bonded to the work.

2. Paint the backer black, using the remaining pattern as a stencil-like mask. Allow to dry.

V. Assemble the Segments.
1. Remove the remaining pattern. Glue the segments, one at a time, to the painted backer, spacing the segments as appropriate. **Note:** Use a "tacky" craft glue if gluing segments to a painted surface. Otherwise use regular white or yellow woodworking glue for gluing raw wood to wood joints.

LUV BUGS
Design by Aaron Moriarity

Enlarge 117% for full-size pattern

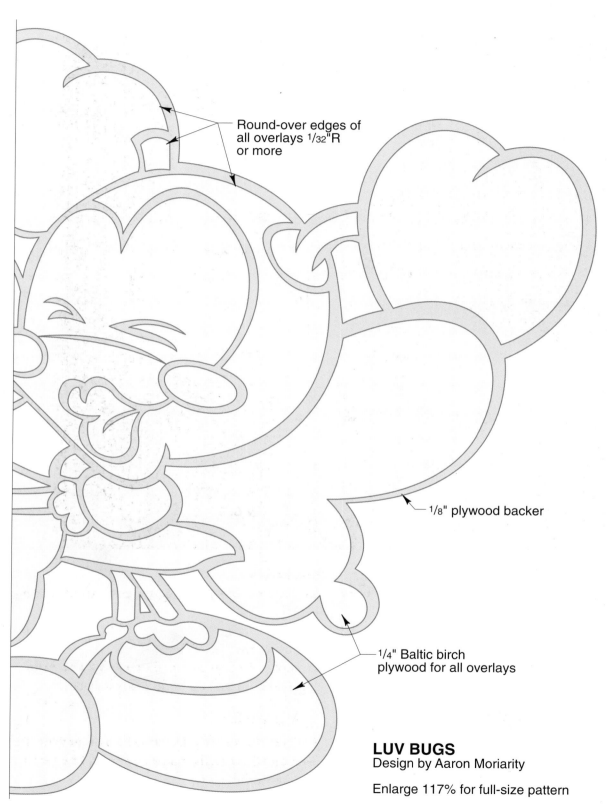

Round-over edges of
all overlays 1/32"R
or more

1/8" plywood backer

1/4" Baltic birch
plywood for all overlays

LUV BUGS
Design by Aaron Moriarity

Enlarge 117% for full-size pattern

Segmented Butterfly

This dimensional Monarch butterfly is a quick and easy project that serves as a constant reminder of the wonders of nature.

Supplies
¾"-thick pine: ¾" x 4"
⅛"-thick plywood: 6½" x 7" (2)
Basic Tools & Supplies from page 15
Wire: 16 gauge

Instructions
See Segmentation Technique Instructions on pages 16–28.

I. Prepare the Patterns.
1. Apply one Segmented Butterfly pattern from pages 111–112 to each piece of plywood.

II. Cut the Wood.
1. Make the 12° beveled surfaces as shown on the Segmented Butterfly pattern on page 112 for the bottom of the body.

2. Cut out the rough shape, using the body compound-sawing patterns. See Photo No. 13-2.

Photo No. 13-2   The butterfly body is cut to rough shape by employing compound scroll sawing techniques. Notice the pattern is centered on the two beveled surfaces.

3. Simultaneously stack-cut the right and left wing. Save the scraps for stack-cutting the overlays.

III. Shape & Smooth the Wood.
1. Round-over the corners to shape the upper surfaces of the body, using a drum sander. See Photo No. 13-3.

Photo No. 13-3   After compound sawing, round-over the corners to give shape to the upper surfaces of the body. The wings are then glued to the flat beveled surfaces.

2. Round-over and slightly contour the wing edges. See Photo No. 13-4.

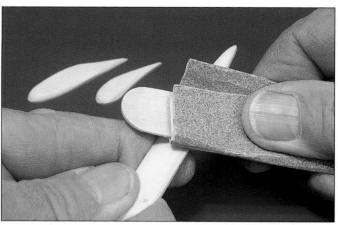

Photo No. 13-4   Shape the edges and surfaces of the ⅛" plywood segment overlays with coarse abrasive paper.

3. Round-over the overlay edges.

4. Drill holes in the body for the wire antennae. Shape the wires and glue them in place.

IV. Color & Finish the Segments.
1. Paint the wings and body flat black.

2. Paint the overlays bright orange.

3. Once the paint has dried, add off-white dots for detail. **Note:** An easy way to do this is by using the pointed handle end of a small paintbrush or a toothpick dipped into the off-white paint. Make the dots just as you would use a pen or pencil to dot the letter "i." Frequently remove the excess paint from the handle so it does not build up and make progressively larger dots.

V. Assemble the Segments.
1. Glue the body to the wings. See Segmented Butterfly pattern on opposite page and end view of the bottom of the body.

VI. Make a Backer
1. Drill a small angular hole part way into the body from the back side and hang the completed piece on a nail.

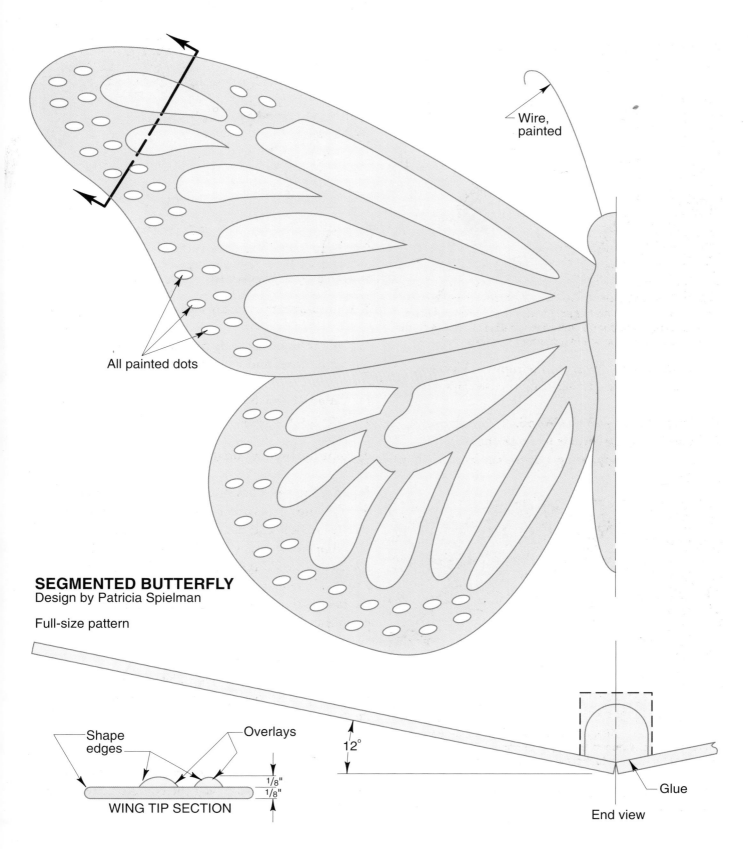

Wire, painted

All painted dots

SEGMENTED BUTTERFLY
Design by Patricia Spielman

Full-size pattern

Shape
edges

Overlays

1/8"
1/8"

WING TIP SECTION

12°

Glue

End view

111

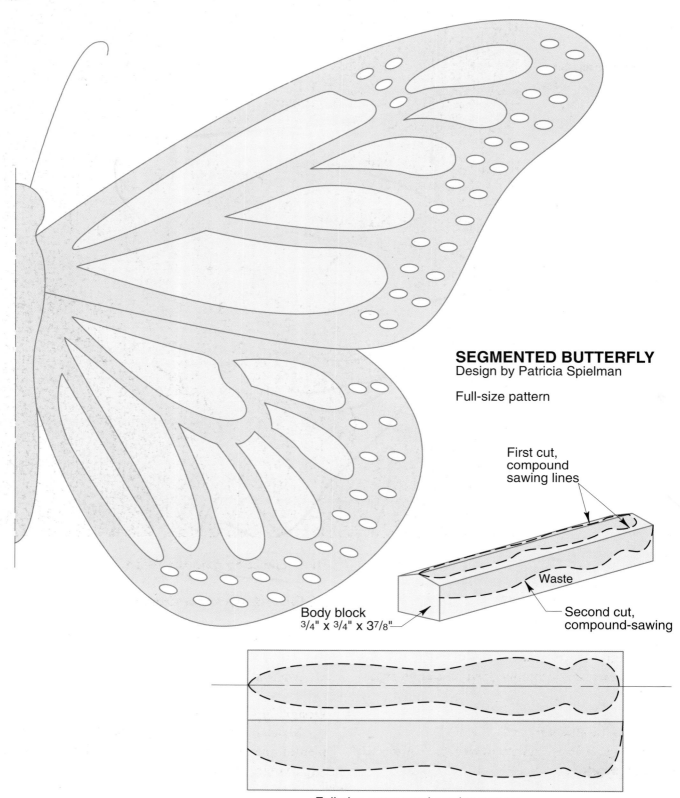

SEGMENTED BUTTERFLY
Design by Patricia Spielman

Full-size pattern

First cut,
compound
sawing lines

Waste

Second cut,
compound-sawing

Body block
3/4" x 3/4" x 3⁷/₈"

Full-size compound-sawing pattern

Viking

Symbolizing the rugged seafaring Scandinavian of centuries past, this is also the perfect symbol for Minnesota professional football fans.

Supplies
¼"-thick plywood: 8½" x 11"
⅛"-thick plywood: 8½" x 11"
Basic Tools & Supplies from page 15

Instructions
See Segmentation Technique Instructions on pages 16–28.

I. Prepare the Patterns.
1. Apply one Viking pattern from page 114 to each piece of plywood.

II. Cut the Wood.

III. Shape & Smooth the Wood.

IV. Color & Finish the Segments.

V. Assemble the Segments.

VI. Make a Backer.

Design Tip
Make a fretwork version of the project by cutting pierced openings instead of overlays without making any changes to the pattern.

VIKING
Design by Patricia Spielman

Enlarge 125% for full-size pattern

Chapter 14
Intarsia Segmentation

Intarsia is a more advanced segmentation technique that is also more challenging and a bit more time consuming. Instead of being constructed from a single piece of wood, intarsia projects are made up of various pieces of wood—each chosen specifically for its natural color as well as its figure, or grain, direction, which complements the general design effect. In this technique, each segment of intarsia is cut individually and must be made to fit precisely against the adjoining segments.

Photo courtesy of Albert F. Winberg

Intarsia Rosebud

This project is a good introduction to intarsia, involving the use of fine hardwoods. The completed piece makes a beautiful wall decoration.

Supplies
¾"-thick padauk: 6" x 7"
¾"-thick poplar: 3" x 6", green-colored
⅛"- to ¼"-thick plywood: 7" x 12"
Basic Tools & Supplies from page 15

Instructions
See Segmentation Technique Instructions on pages 16–28.

I. Prepare the Patterns.
1. See the Intarsia Rosebud pattern on page 116 for information pertaining to recommended species, sizes, and directions.

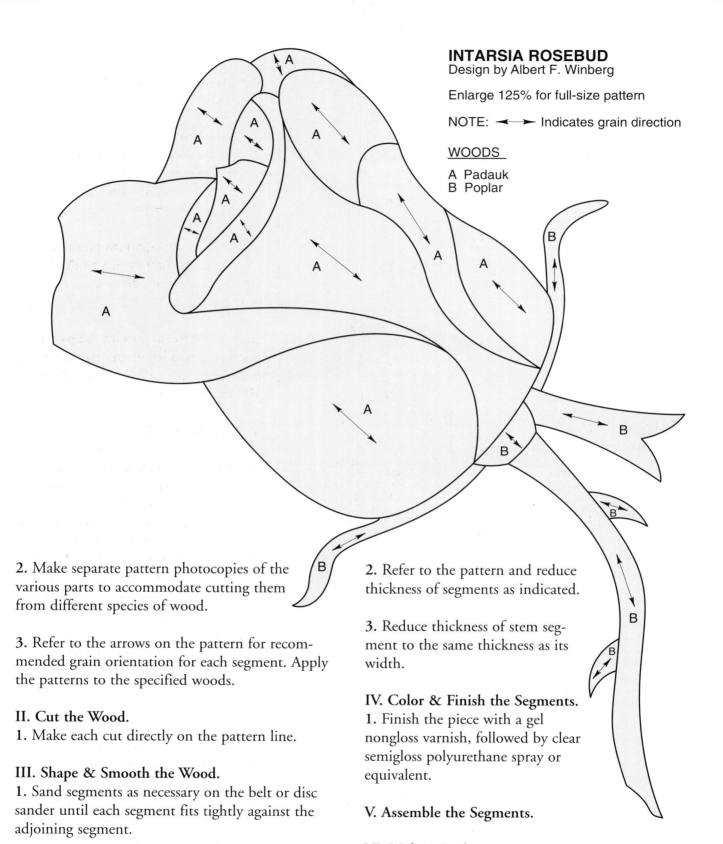

INTARSIA ROSEBUD
Design by Albert F. Winberg

Enlarge 125% for full-size pattern

NOTE: ◄—► Indicates grain direction

<u>WOODS</u>

A Padauk
B Poplar

2. Make separate pattern photocopies of the various parts to accommodate cutting them from different species of wood.

3. Refer to the arrows on the pattern for recommended grain orientation for each segment. Apply the patterns to the specified woods.

II. Cut the Wood.
1. Make each cut directly on the pattern line.

III. Shape & Smooth the Wood.
1. Sand segments as necessary on the belt or disc sander until each segment fits tightly against the adjoining segment.

2. Refer to the pattern and reduce thickness of segments as indicated.

3. Reduce thickness of stem segment to the same thickness as its width.

IV. Color & Finish the Segments.
1. Finish the piece with a gel nongloss varnish, followed by clear semigloss polyurethane spray or equivalent.

V. Assemble the Segments.

VI. Make a Backer.

Intarsia Santa

Supplies
¾"-thick maple: 6" x 6½"
¾"-thick paduak: 8" x 11"
¾"-thick walnut: 3" x 8"
⅛"- to ¼"-thick plywood: 8" x 12½"
Basic Tools & Supplies from page 15

Instructions
See Segmentation Technique Instructions on pages 16–28.

I. Prepare the Patterns.
1. See the Intarsia Santa pattern on pages 118–119 for information pertaining to recommended species, sizes, and directions.

2. Make separate pattern photocopies of the various parts to accommodate cutting them from different species of wood.

3. Refer to the arrows on the pattern for recommended grain orientation for each segment. Apply the patterns to the specified woods.

II. Cut the Wood.

III. Shape & Smooth the Wood.
1. Prepare ⅛" and ¼" plywood shims for those segments to be elevated as specified on the pattern. The lower fur rim of the cap will show the shim material at the outside edges. Prepare and fit this shim material from the same wood material as the cap rim so it is less noticeable.

IV. Color & Finish the Segments.
1. Paint each triangular-shaped eye segment blue and black with a small dot of white.

2. To achieve the white look, thin white acrylic paint or use a white pickling stain. **Note:** Oil stains will wipe off easier but they will take differently on softwoods than hardwoods. Be certain to test stains and special finishes on scrap to be certain you are satisfied with the results before using them on your project.

V. Assemble the Segments.

VI. Make a Backer.

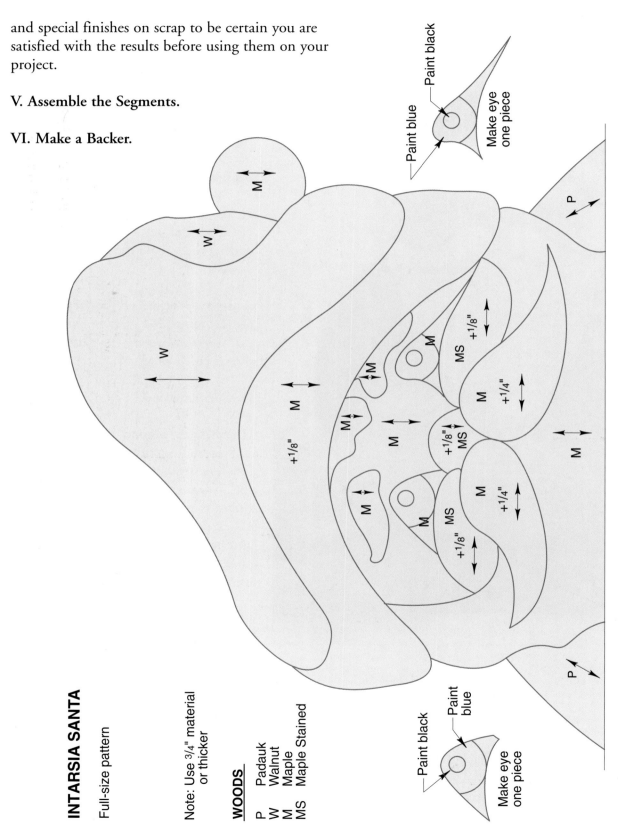

INTARSIA SANTA

Full-size pattern

Note: Use 3/4" material or thicker

WOODS

P Padauk
W Walnut
M Maple
MS Maple Stained

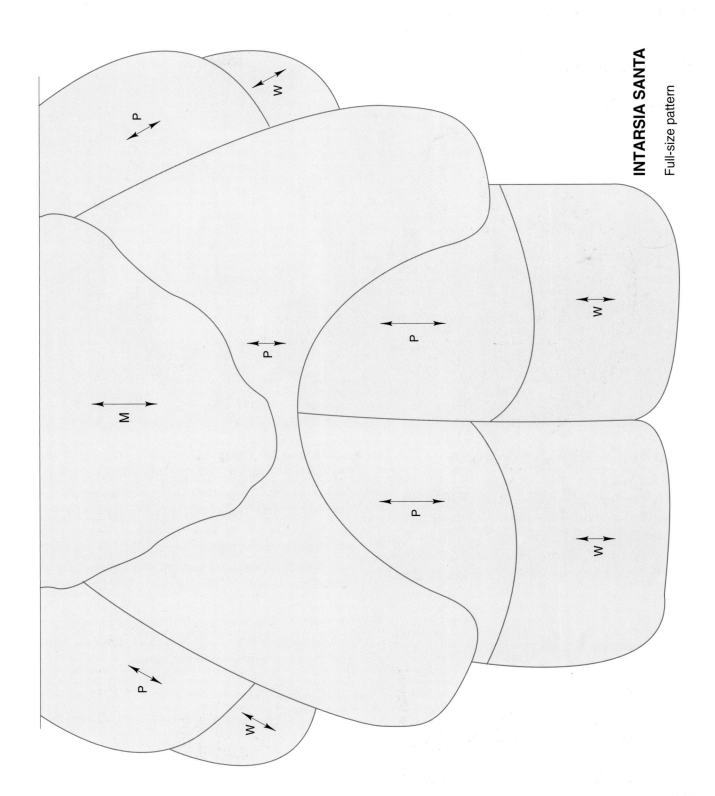

INTARSIA SANTA

Full-size pattern

Umbrella Man & Woman

Here are two easy intarsia projects that will delight and humor all those who see them. These are two among many original designs created by intarsia artist Albert F. Winberg. These particular designs were inspired by the doodling his daughter did as a child.

Supplies
¾"-thick western cedar: 17½" x 15"
⅛"- to ¼"-thick plywood: 17½" x 21"
Basic Tools & Supplies from page 15
Miscellaneous other woods

Instructions
See Segmentation Technique Instructions on pages 16–28.

I. Prepare the Patterns.
1. See the Umbrella Man & Woman pattern on pages 121–122 for information pertaining to recommended species, sizes, and directions.

2. Make separate pattern photocopies of the various parts to accommodate cutting them from different species of wood.

3. Refer to the arrows on the pattern for recommended grain orientation for each segment. Apply the patterns to the specified woods.

II. Cut the Wood.
1. Make each cut directly on the pattern line.

III. Shape & Smooth the Wood.
1. Sand segments as necessary on the belt or disc

sander until each segment fits tightly against the adjoining segment.

IV. Color & Finish the Segments.
1. Finish the piece with a gel nongloss varnish, followed by clear semigloss polyurethane spray or equivalent.

V. Assemble the Segments.
1. Glue the nose segments on.

2. Set the eyes and mouth segments, which are made from thinner wood than the surrounding stock, into openings cut with the scroll saw.

VI. Make a Backer.

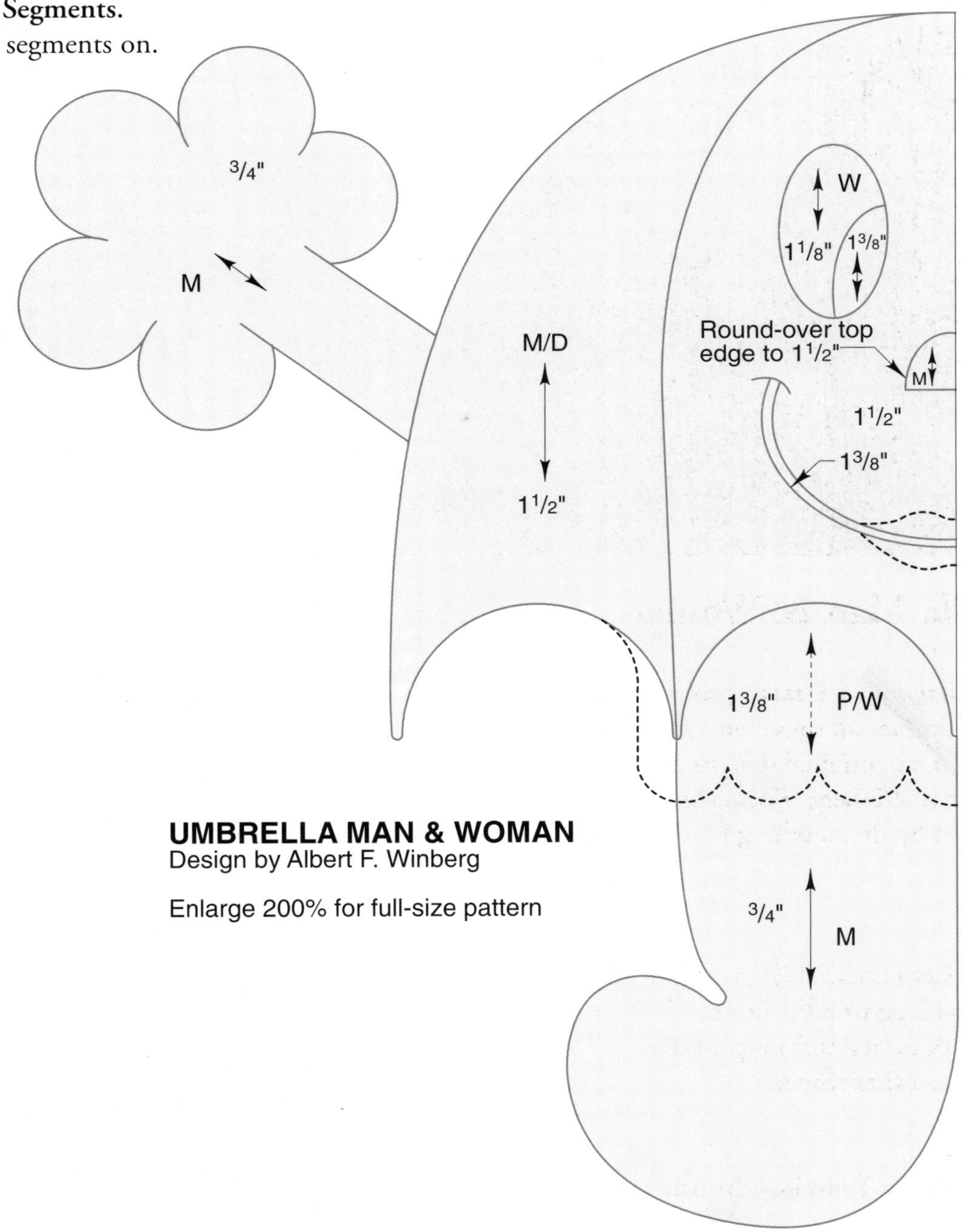

3/4"

M

M/D

1 1/2"

W

1 1/8" 1 3/8"

Round-over top edge to 1 1/2"

M

1 1/2"

1 3/8"

1 3/8" P/W

UMBRELLA MAN & WOMAN
Design by Albert F. Winberg

Enlarge 200% for full-size pattern

3/4" M

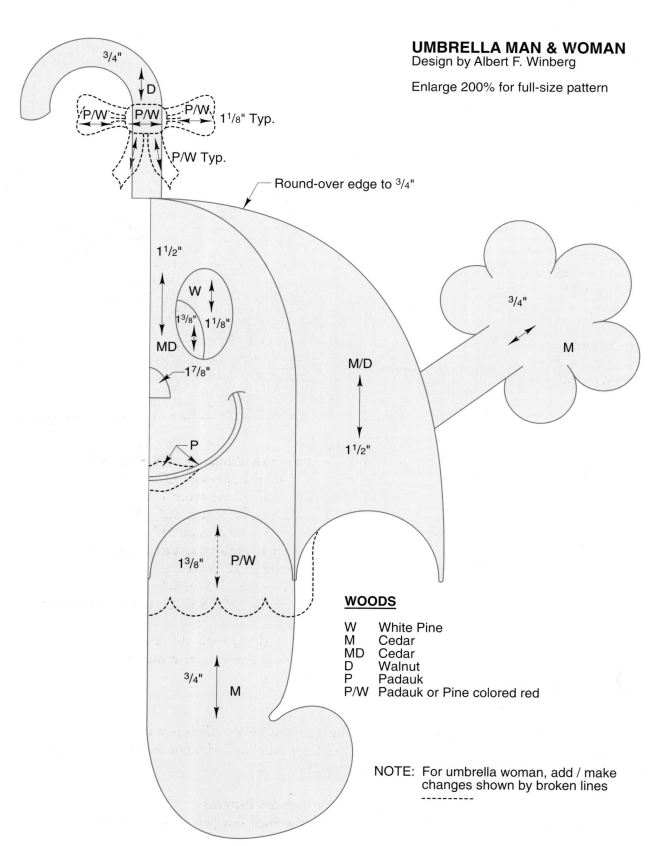

UMBRELLA MAN & WOMAN
Design by Albert F. Winberg

Enlarge 200% for full-size pattern

3/4"

D

P/W   P/W   P/W   1⅛" Typ.

P/W Typ.

Round-over edge to 3/4"

1½"

W

1³⁄₈"   1⅛"

MD

1⁷⁄₈"

P

M/D

1½"

3/4"

M

1³⁄₈"   P/W

3/4"   M

WOODS

W   White Pine
M   Cedar
MD   Cedar
D   Walnut
P   Padauk
P/W Padauk or Pine colored red

NOTE: For umbrella woman, add / make
changes shown by broken lines

Shell Box

The intarsia Shell Box, as designed and crafted by Joan West, requires seven different species of wood. This same project could, however, be made entirely from one species.

Joan's flock-lined compartments are made to fit her sewing implements. Notice the flocked design on the inside of the lid and the short retaining chain that restricts the hinging of the lid.

Supplies

³⁄₁₆"- to ¾"-thick afromosia: 3" x 8"; 8" x 7"
³⁄₁₆"- to ¾"-thick basswood: 12" x 8¾"
³⁄₁₆"- to ¾"-thick bloodwood: 4" x 4¾"
³⁄₁₆"- to ¾"-thick lacewood: 3¼" x 11"
³⁄₁₆"- to ¾"-thick tulipwood: 1½" x 5"
³⁄₁₆"-thick ebony: miscellaneous small pieces
½"-thick walnut: 12" x 8¾"
⁵⁄₁₆"-thick basswood: 12" x 8¾"
¼"-thick cordia: 12" x 8¾" (2); miscellaneous small
    pieces
⅛"- to ¼"-thick plywood: 8¾" x 12"
Basic Tools & Supplies from page 15
Chain
Hinges (2)

Instructions for the Shell Box Lid

See Segmentation Technique Instructions on pages 16–28.

I. Prepare the Patterns.

1. See the Shell Box pattern on pages 125–126 for

information pertaining to recommended species, sizes, and directions.

2. Make separate pattern photocopies of the various parts to accommodate cutting them from different species of wood.

3. Refer to the arrows on the pattern for recommended grain orientation for each segment. Apply the patterns to the specified woods.

II. Cut the Wood.
1. Make each cut directly on the pattern line.

2. First, cut the long central segment of the shell. Cut and fit the adjoining segments to it as you work each way toward the hinge locations. **Note:** It is easier to make the edge of an outside curve fit against a segment with an inside curved edge. Careful cutting should keep fitting to a minimum.

III. Shape & Smooth the Wood.
1. Sand segments as necessary on the belt or disc sander until each segment fits tightly against the adjoining segment.

2. Round-over all edges, using a combination of hand tools and high-speed rotary tools. **Note:** The segments that flow and separate into two forms are the most difficult to shape. Work slowly and always push the knife or chisel edges with the grain. See Photo 14-1. Sand each piece smoothly.

Photo No. 14-1   Here, a structured carbide rotary burr forms a v-groove. This is a preliminary step to blending the intersection of two rounded edges.

124

VI. Make a Backer. & V. Assemble the Segments
1. First, glue down the longer central segments, then the band, and then the remaining segments, working from the center toward the hinge area on each side. **Note:** Portions of the backer will be exposed in the areas between the hinges and the ends of the band.

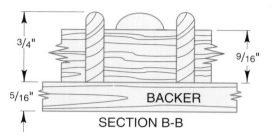

SECTION B-B

IV. Color & Finish the Segments.
1. Flock or paint the underside of the lid as desired.

2. Apply a gel nongloss varnish, followed by clear semigloss polyurethane spray or equivalent.

Instructions for the Shell Box

I. Prepare the Patterns.
1. Stack and glue one or more thicknesses of various woods together.

2. Apply one Shell Box pattern from pages 125–126 to the top layer of stacked woods.

II. Cut the Wood.
1. Cut the Shell Box wall from the stacked and glued layers.

2. Place and cut individual profile-shaped outlines, with a total thickness of slightly more than the overall height of the sewing implement, through one or more layers of wood.

III. Shape & Smooth the Wood.
1. Sand as necessary on the belt or disc sander.

VII. Make a Box Bottom.
1. Make a bottom. See Section A-A on the Shell Box pattern on page 126.

2. Glue the box wall to the bottom.

3. Bevel back the edge of the bottom.

IV. Color & Finish the Segments.
1. Flock or paint the inside of the box.

2. Apply a gel nongloss varnish, followed by clear semigloss polyurethane spray or equivalent.

3. Add the hinges and a short length of chain for a lid stop.

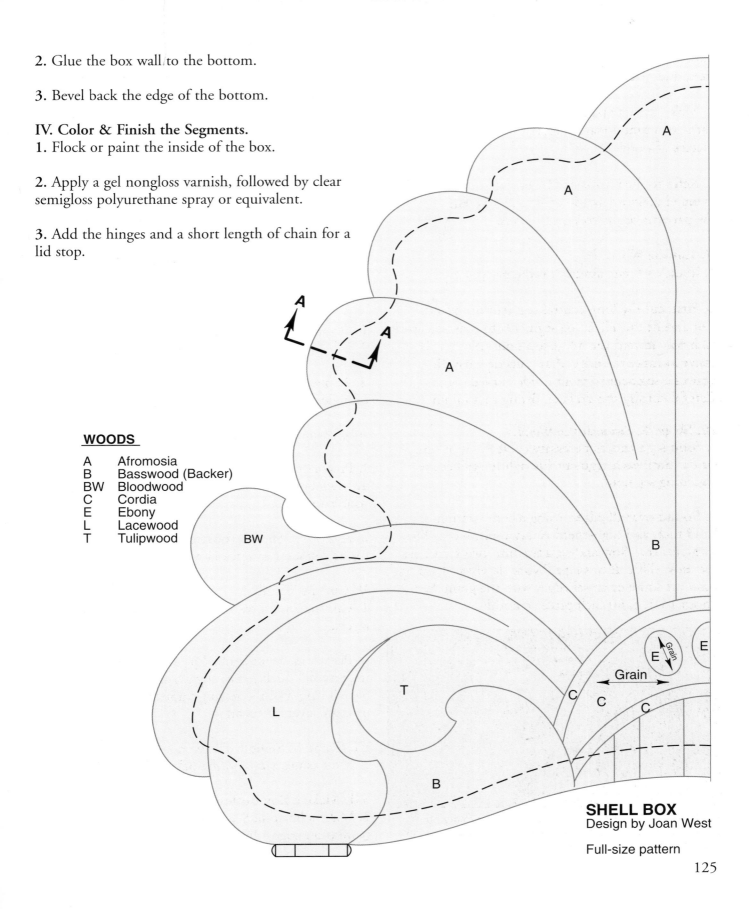

WOODS

A	Afromosia
B	Basswood (Backer)
BW	Bloodwood
C	Cordia
E	Ebony
L	Lacewood
T	Tulipwood

SHELL BOX
Design by Joan West

Full-size pattern

125

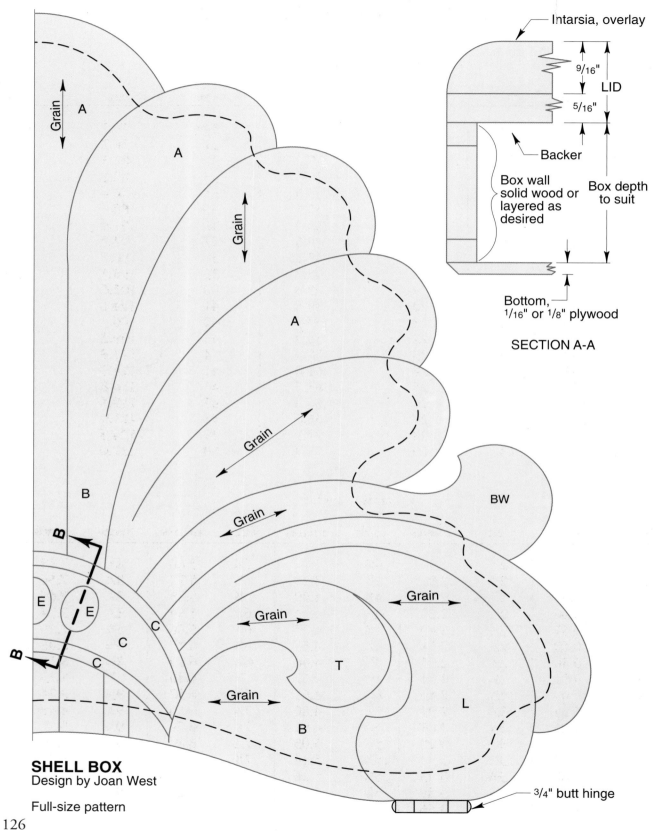

Intarsia, overlay

9/16"
LID
5/16"

Backer

Box wall
solid wood or
layered as
desired

Box depth
to suit

Bottom,
1/16" or 1/8" plywood

SECTION A-A

Grain

A

A

Grain

A

Grain

Grain

B

BW

B

E

E

C

Grain

Grain

C

C

Grain

T

Grain

C

L

Grain

B

B

SHELL BOX
Design by Joan West

Full-size pattern

126

3/4" butt hinge

Metric Equivalency Chart

mm-millimetres   cm-centimetres
inches to millimetres and centimetres

inches	mm	cm	inches	cm	inches	cm
⅛	3	0.3	9	22.9	30	76.2
¼	6	0.6	10	25.4	31	78.7
⅜	10	1.0	11	27.9	32	81.3
½	13	1.3	12	30.5	33	83.8
⅝	16	1.6	13	33.0	34	86.4
¾	19	1.9	14	35.6	35	88.9
⅞	22	2.2	15	38.1	36	91.4
1	25	2.5	16	40.6	37	94.0
1¼	32	3.2	17	43.2	38	96.5
1½	38	3.8	18	45.7	39	99.1
1¾	44	4.4	19	48.3	40	101.6
2	51	5.1	20	50.8	41	104.1
2½	64	6.4	21	53.3	42	106.7
3	76	7.6	22	55.9	43	109.2
3½	89	8.9	23	58.4	44	111.8
4	102	10.2	24	61.0	45	114.3
4½	114	11.4	25	63.5	46	116.8
5	127	12.7	26	66.0	47	119.4
6	152	15.2	27	68.6	48	121.9
7	178	17.8	28	71.1	49	124.5
8	203	20.3	29	73.7	50	127.0

yards to metres

yards	metres	yards	metres	yards	metres	yards	metres	yards	metres
⅛	0.11	2⅛	1.94	4⅛	3.77	6⅛	5.60	8⅛	7.43
¼	0.23	2¼	2.06	4¼	3.89	6¼	5.72	8¼	7.54
⅜	0.34	2⅜	2.17	4⅜	4.00	6⅜	5.83	8⅜	7.66
½	0.46	2½	2.29	4½	4.11	6½	5.94	8½	7.77
⅝	0.57	2⅝	2.40	4⅝	4.23	6⅝	6.06	8⅝	7.89
¾	0.69	2¾	2.51	4¾	4.34	6¾	6.17	8¾	8.00
⅞	0.80	2⅞	2.63	4⅞	4.46	6⅞	6.29	8⅞	8.12
1	0.91	3	2.74	5	4.57	7	6.40	9	8.23
1⅛	1.03	3⅛	2.86	5⅛	4.69	7⅛	6.52	9⅛	8.34
1¼	1.14	3¼	2.97	5¼	4.80	7¼	6.63	9¼	8.46
1⅜	1.26	3⅜	3.09	5⅜	4.91	7⅜	6.74	9⅜	8.57
1½	1.37	3½	3.20	5½	5.03	7½	6.86	9½	8.69
1⅝	1.49	3⅝	3.31	5⅝	5.14	7⅝	6.97	9⅝	8.80
1¾	1.60	3¾	3.43	5¾	5.26	7¾	7.09	9¾	8.92
1⅞	1.71	3⅞	3.54	5⅞	5.37	7⅞	7.20	9⅞	9.03
2	1.83	4	3.66	6	5.49	8	7.32	10	9.14

Index

A–B

Advantages of Segmentation.................7
Angel.................55
Antique Anchor.................75
Assemble the Segments.................27
Basic Techniques & Tools.................14
Basic Tools & Supplies.................15
Big Catch.................86
Blades.................10

C

Carved Duck.................39
Chapter 1.................8
Chapter 2.................12
Chapter 3.................14
Chapter 4: Segmented Fish.................29
Chapter 5: Segmented Birds.................35
Chapter 6: Halloween & Thanksgiving.................49
Chapter 7: Christmas.................53
Chapter 8: Fantasy.................61
Chapter 9: Nautical Projects.................70
Chapter 10: Nostalgic Projects.................84
Chapter 11: Country Projects.................91
Chapter 12: Home Decor.................101
Chapter 13: Separated Segmentation.................106
Chapter 14: Intarsia Segmentation.................115
Color & Finish the Segments.................26
Cut the Wood.................16

D–I

Duck Decoy.................41
First Kiss.................84
Four-piece Sea Gull.................37
Heart in Home.................102
Holiday Turkey.................51
Intarsia Rosebud.................115
Intarsia Santa.................117
Introduction.................6

L–N

Lighthouse.................72
Luv Bugs.................106

Madonna & Child.................59
Make a Backer.................28
Making Rope-edged Plaques.................80
Mermaid.................70
Metric Equivalency Chart.................127
Moon Face.................64
Nativity.................57

P–R

Pink & Blue Fish.................31
Plywood & Sheet Materials.................13
Prepare the Patterns.................16
Prepare the Saw.................15
Proceed with Safety.................14
Pumpkin & Ghost.................49
Road Runner.................45
Rooster Plaques.................93

S

Santa Face.................53
Scroll Saws.................8
Sculpted Sailboat.................78
Segmentation Technique Instructions.................16
Segmentation versus Intarsia.................6
Segmented Butterfly.................109
Segmented Mirror.................104
Segmented Pony.................99
Segmented Sunflower.................96
Small Rooster.................91
Shape & Smooth the Wood.................18
Shell Box.................123
Speckled Fish.................33
Striped Fish.................29
Sun Face.................61
Swan.................43

T–W

Two-piece Shore Bird.................35
Umbrella Man & Woman.................120
Unicorn.................67
Viking.................113
Woman with Basket.................89
Wood Materials.................12